C000121580

The Sporting Gun's Bedside Companion

Also by Douglas Butler

Rough Shooting in Ireland

Wild Duck and their Pursuit

The Sporting Gun's Bedside Companion

Douglas Butler

and friends

MERLIN UNWIN BOOKS

First published in Great Britain by Merlin Unwin Books, 2012
Text © Douglas Butler, 2012

Published by:

Merlin Unwin Books Ltd
Palmers House
7 Corve Street
Ludlow
Shropshire SY8 1DB U.K.
www.merlinunwin.co.uk

The author asserts his moral right to be identified with this work.
Designed and set in Bembo by Merlin Unwin.
Printed in the UK by TJ International Ltd, Padstow, Cornwall.

ISBN 978-1-906122-48-5

DEDICATION
To Margaret

Contents

Acknowledgements

There is an extraordinarily wide range of shooting traditions. For one man his sport centres on farmland and coaxing pheasants from frosty autumnal hedgerows, for another it is all about the hard slog across scrub and bog in search of woodcock and snipe. For others the main focus is on the changing light over salt marsh and mudflats or the pursuit on heathery uplands of the real king of our game birds. Down the years I have been more than privileged to drink well and often from the magic cup.

The stories in this book are essentially reflections of great days in great places, the birds that dwell in them and, all important, the companionship of like-minded people. To all those with whom I have shared these times I offer my grateful thanks.

When I set out on this enterprise, not without considerable foreboding I might add as I had never previously attempted to write short stories about shooting, it struck me that the book would benefit from contributions other than simply mine. As a result I asked a number of people to provide stories based upon their personal experiences. To a man and woman they agreed and for this I record my grateful thanks to my son, Rupert, my cousin-in-law (if such term exists!) Nancy Walsh and to my good friends John Bourke, Michael Gately, Seamus Leahy and Anthony O'Halloran. Each, I believe, has made a unique and interesting contribution.

From time to time I find it necessary to get a precise translation of some obscure Irish word. One man has always come up with the goods. That man is Billy O'Dwyer of Clonmel. To him my very special thanks for his unfailing help and courtesy.

Last, but by no means least, a very special thank you to Merlin, Karen and Jo at Merlin Unwin Books. As long as I have known them they have been helpful, supportive and kindness personified. To each my very grateful thanks.

Douglas Butler, 2012

1

Pawel, the hare
and other matters

DURING THE EARLY 1960s we were living and working near a small village in Buckinghamshire. I was billeted in a house at the very edge of the village and Martin was renting a cottage in the grounds of what might loosely be described as a small mansion. The owner was a remarkable Polish gentleman named Pawel. He was one of that heroic band of cavalrymen who, in 1939, had tried to defend their homeland in the face of the German blitzkrieg. In the course of that brief engagement Pawel had been severely wounded. Having recovered from his wounds he continued to live in Poland until it was 'liberated' by the Red Army. At this juncture he had, like so many of his colleagues, made his way to England. When we got to know him he was living in semi-retirement exercising his not inconsiderable literary skills.

In that part of Buckinghamshire there was not a lot of shooting available. The broad tracts of beech woodland were gloomy and inhospitable places and the surrounding fields, largely given over to cereal growing, were in the hands of syndicates. A reasonable scattering of wild pheasants was to be found along the woodland fringes and these were augmented each autumn by moderate release programmes. The grey partridge was still quite plentiful in the area and its unique 'keevit' call was a familiar sound in the gathering dusk. But wild ducks were a very scarce commodity indeed. This was quite high and well-drained land. Ponds were few and far between and the river, some ten miles away, was the nearest source of mallard.

By great good fortune we had been befriended by a local farmer who allowed us to shoot over his lands. Some years previously a syndicate had the shooting of the farm but had succeeded in blotting its copy book. We never discovered what had gone wrong but, as the saying goes, one man's loss is another man's gain. In terms of the general area it was a smallish farm, little over one hundred acres. However it incorporated a small overgrown copse near its centre which held a reasonable number of pheasants and the odd woodcock when the weather turned harsh. Then, less than a mile away, was Three Corner Wood, a conifer plantation owned by our employees. As its name indicated, it was roughly triangular. It was bounded on two sides by quiet country lanes and on the third by a relatively busy road. The wood was bisected by a broad grassy ride from which a number of smaller rides extended at right angles. The great beauty of Three Corner Wood, at least from our point of view, was that pheasants from the surrounding shoots clearly regarded it in the five star category when it came to the matter of roosting quarter. Alas the wood is now no more. Paying a nostalgic visit to the place a few years ago I was saddened to see that a dual carriageway had been driven through it, leaving no more than a few isolated stands of spruce and pine at its extremities. Such, we are told, is the price of that ephemeral commodity called progress.

One evening in late autumn we were sitting by a roaring fire in the local hostelry enjoying a pre-prandial drink with Pawel and his wife. He was in a reflective frame of mind and was reminiscing about the old days in his native Poland. The conversation turned to the subject of food and Pawel confided that one of the dishes he missed most from his childhood days was jugged hare. This surprised me somewhat as hares were quite plentiful in the area and there could have been little difficulty in getting one from a game dealer. However he did not explain why he had not followed this apparently logical course of action. As so often happens with pub conversation, a combination of the demon drink and the warmth of a good fire can trigger a change in the direction of a conversation with quite remarkable rapidity.

Anyway, some days later we were shooting in Three Corner Wood. It was one of those wild wet days when pheasants are not inclined to stir far from their roosts. This suited us just fine as once they departed the wood they quickly entered forbidden territory. We had three or four in the bag and were thinking of calling it a day when a hare broke from a clearing adjoining the central ride. This was not a particularly uncommon event and it was our custom to grant safe passage. I grew up in a place where coursing, both open and park, were afforded the same degree of veneration which rugby football enjoys in the Welsh valleys. In consequence we never regarded hares as fair game. They were another man's sport and that was the end of the matter. Indeed it would have been considered little short of sacrilege to turn a gun on one.

But, as the hare accelerated away, the conversation with Pawel a few days earlier came to mind. Before the report of my gun had died away – woods are great places for echoes – the hare had completed a double somersault and lay dead at the edge of the ride. I had never carried a hare before and this seemed to me to be a substantial beast. I was quite convinced that it would tip the scales at somewhere around the one stone mark though, realistically, it probably weighed little more than seven or eight pounds.

Later that evening I delivered the hare chez Pawel. Happily for me, as subsequent events would prove, he and his good lady wife were not at home. This left me with something of a dilemma as Pawel's home usually had a few cats in residence. Quite clearly the hare could not be parked just anywhere. Fortunately a bracket designed to support a hanging basket during the summer months was strategically situated by the back door well above cat range.

Next day Pawel phoned to thank me for the hare. For a man who rarely displayed much in the way of emotion he was clearly very touched by my gift. Maybe it was because it brought back memories of his home place of long ago. Martin and I, he insisted, together with our lady friends, must join them for dinner the following Saturday evening.

Entering Pawel's house at the appointed hour it was immediately apparent, even to the most uneducated of nostrils, that hare was on the menu. The air positively reeked with the smell of the simmering beast. A pre-dinner drink, or more accurately multiple drinks, was first on the agenda. Vodka was the prescribed medicine. Sitting at the fire the assembled company imbibed freely of the colourless spirit. Indeed, my legs were rather less than steady when we eventually made for the dining room.

At this juncture, I must confess, memory is rather less than perfect. There was a large mahogany table, a lot of fine silverware and quite a lot of bottles of vodka. Of such I am sure. Of subsequent matters pertaining to that evening I am far from certain. Of consuming the hare, for example, I have no memory whatsoever. Of getting home I have a vague recollection of using the white line along the centre of the road for navigational purposes. Martin of course was rather more lucky. He had merely to cross the lawn to get to his cottage.

The evening was not without its repercussions. We never saw the two lady friends again. Not surprising, some may think, given the circumstances. As to vodka, the evil liquid has never since passed my lips. Nor ever will it. And, as for hare, I have never shot one since. Nor ever will I.

2

The white-front that wouldn't go away

TOM HAD BEEN a member of the syndicate for a long number of years. He was a quiet and affable man who was passionate about his sport and a firm favourite with the other members. His knowledge of the creatures of the wild and their ways was little short of encyclo-paedic. And, it must be added, he was no mean performer with the gun. Accompanied by his black Labrador, Teal, Tom was nearly always the first to put in an appearance on the morning of a shoot. Teal figures prominently in this narrative so it is only right and proper that he too be afforded a formal introduction. Four years old, big as Labradors go and strong as the proverbial ox, he had already earned for himself something of a reputation in the retrieving department. Persistence was his essential trademark. On many occasions much to the chagrin of their masters, he had arrived back with the goods after lesser hounds had given up the search.

The syndicate in question was a wildfowling one which, like a number of others, operated in the vicinity of Wexford Harbour. This area of low-lying land in the south-east corner of Ireland has long been a Mecca for wildfowlers. Ducks of many species are to be found in the harbour and on the adjacent Sloblands, two polders reclaimed from the sea in the 1800s. Waders too are very plentiful and their swirling flocks do much to entertain wildfowlers during lulls in the shooting. But this is a story about geese, or more correctly, one particular wild goose. Greylags, once very numerous, had all but deserted the harbour when Tom joined the syndicate in the 1960s. The majority opinion was that they had moved their wintering grounds to the east of Scotland where the big attraction was an ever-increasing acreage of barley stubbles. As far as I am aware Tom never shot one there. They had, however, been replaced by White-fronts and over the years he had certainly taken his toll of these wild and wary visitors from Greenland.

1982 was a sad year for Irish wildfowlers. As a result of what would prove to be the most unreliable of population figures a ban on the shooting of Greenland White-fronts was introduced. The syndicate had thus to content itself with the pursuit of ducks and a rather different shooting regime. Before the ban was brought in, Tom and his colleagues would be suitably concealed in hides or reed beds well before dawn. From these points of ambush they would then concentrate on duck such as wigeon and mallard with the coming of the new day. Then, an hour or so after dawn, the White-fronts would lift from the sand bars on which they had roosted and head for stubbles or grassy fields. Duck shooting, not surprisingly, would now quickly cease. Grossly unfair to teal and their ilk no doubt, considering the variety of challenges they can provide, but what wildfowler in his right mind would open up on them when the immediate future promised a better-than-evens chance of a right and left at White-fronts? Now, however, the geese were assured of safe passage and the morning was devoted solely to duck.

The ban had only been in operation for a couple of months when, on a wild and wet December morning, Tom and his friends assembled as usual in that blackness that precedes the dawn. The wind, not far short of gale force, was almost due east, a direction which greatly favoured his hide. Effectively the duck would be forced to follow the line of the reed beds that concealed his hide and pass almost directly over his head.

On very wet mornings duck can be slow to take to the wing

and the dawn is often well advanced before shooting can begin. This particular morning, however, was one of the exceptions. Whilst it was still too dark to pick up the familiar silhouettes, the familiar sound of wings overhead during lulls in the gale indicated that substantial numbers were already on the move. On one occasion Tom thought that he heard the laughing cackle of a White-front but as it was so blustery he concluded that his ears had deceived him. Little did he realise at that moment just how well-tuned his ears really were.

Minutes later the action began in earnest. The crackle of gunfire a hundred yards or so upwind alerted Tom to coming events. Within a few seconds, three duck appeared out of the glooming. They were large, almost certainly mallard, and travelling at knots with the wind in their tails. Little more than sixty feet above the water, the trio had passed the hide before he was able to line up the leading bird. At the shot, it duly crumpled and Teal was already off to make the retrieve: he had spotted the duck well before his master. There was no time for a second barrel. The wind had already whipped the two survivors away into the security of the semi-darkness. As Tom was taking the mallard from Teal, he picked up movement out of the corner of his eye. An ever-vigilant duck was flying high and would have survived but for a fatal error. It turned and tried in vain to make good its escape into the wind. Once again Teal did the necessary.

With black clouds scurrying across the eastern sky, dawn was making extremely slow progress. A small pack of teal appeared, only to disappear again before Tom's gun had reached his shoulder. Almost immediately another single bird crossed high from behind providing him with a half chance. Tom's gun was already mounted and it took only a minor adjustment to cover the latest arrival. Once again Teal was in the water before the echo of the shot had died away.

What happened next was most certainly not on Tom's agenda for the day. As Teal swam towards the hide, the duck secured in his mouth seemed to be, for lack of a better description, rather on the large side. And indeed it was. Mortified, Tom found himself presented with a White-front. A decent man who had made an honest mistake, he now found himself with something of a dilemma. Never before had he shot a bird out of season or, for that matter, a protected one. What was he to do? Taking it back to the car at the end of the morning did not, quite frankly, seem like a good idea. Secure and discrete disposal appeared to be his best option. Looking around he noticed a large clump of gorse and brambles not too far away. This clump would be his salvation. Shielding the goose beneath his jacket, he made for the piece of cover. Then, obscured from prying eyes by a large bush, he hurled the goose into the densest part of the cover. There, he hoped it would remain, safely concealed until some marauding fox or badger found it. Tom then returned to his hide. Still perturbed by this turn of events, he was scarcely back when two shots rang out from a neighbouring hide. Teal, undoubtedly confused by his master's strange behaviour, was gone like a flash. He was soon to return with the White-front, now in less than pristine condition.

Disposal was once again on the agenda. Returning to the cover, Tom located a recently excavated rabbit burrow. This, he thought, might be the answer to his problem. The goose was duly stuffed down the hole, a full arm's length. He then sighed the obligatory sigh of relief and returned again to his hide. Unfortunately, Teal, now more than ever confused by his master's errant behaviour, was not prepared to engage in such subterfuge. At the next volley of shots he was gone again. And this time rather slower to return. But when he finally did, it was all too apparent what he had been at. His snout and paws were liberally dusted with damp red clay and the object in his mouth was just about recognisable as being a creature of the feathered persuasion. At this juncture a lesser man would probably have shot the dog. But such was not in Tom's nature. The goose was returned to its crypt which was then sealed with a large rock. This should have been the end of the matter.

Teal, however, was not a dog that could be accused of throwing in the towel. Once again he disappeared in response to nearby shooting and after a rather lengthy period of time had elapsed, duly delivered the bedraggled remains of the goose to Tom once more.

Clearly a battle of wits had been joined in earnest. Back to the rabbit burrow once more. The bird was pushed in even deeper with a long stick and the hole was filled with sufficient stones to fill a small trailer. And Teal was the recipient of an extremely stern warning as to his future conduct.

That was effectively the end of the matter as far as the goose was concerned but Tom still faced a final hurdle. His trips to the cover could not have gone unnoticed. Like many a good fighter before him, he reckoned that the best policy was to get his retaliation in first. Arriving back at the car later in the morning he confided to his colleagues that for the first time he could remember, Teal had failed to make a retrieve. 'I think that it was a wigeon,' he said, 'but I couldn't be certain, it was still quite dark. I know that it fell near that patch of bushes behind the hide. I took Teal over a couple of times but there was no sign of it. Perhaps it got up again.'

3

Contrasting fortunes

IT HAD BEEN some drive and they could certainly do without this. The trio had left Gloucester early on Saturday afternoon and driven through the night. Now, at 7.00am, they were left with no alternative but to sit and wait. Jim, who had wakened a couple of hours earlier to take his turn at the wheel, was decidedly groggy. All he wanted was to get to the hotel and go to bed. The fact that his 18-year-old son, Robbie, was curled up fast asleep on the back seat, clearly oblivious to everything, did little to improve his humour. His long-term shooting companion, Philip, was almost equally groggy. Initially delighted to be able to sit back and close his eyes after driving for three hours, he was literally too tired to go to sleep.

The car ferry was the problem. Or, more specifically, the fact that it was tied up and had every appearance of remaining in that position for the foreseeable future. Ever since a mutual friend had recommended a small hotel on the Isle of Skye, every aspect of the trip had been the subject of meticulous planning. This was to be a grouse shooting trip with a difference. So they thought. Right now here they were at the Kyle of Lochalsh and here, it would seem, they were destined to stay. This, I must hasten to add, was before the Skye bridge had been built and travellers were reliant upon the good offices of the ferry company. It had simply not occurred to the three Sassenachs that the timetable operating for the Sabbath would be considerably more restricted than was the case for the rest of the week. Nothing for it so but to give Jim's pointer, Flint, a run and admire the rugged scenery until they could resume their journey.

Eventually the sea was crossed and nearly 24 hours after leaving home, the weary group reached its destination. Amazing though how thoughts of marsh, moor and mountain affect the psyche of the shooting man. The ardours of the long journey were quickly forgotten, aided, it has to be admitted, by a few shots of mountain dew. The focus was now firmly on the morrow and, hopefully, the great things it would bring. The hotel held a long lease over a considerable area of moor and mountain which was divided up into a number of beats. A rota system operated so that each group was allotted a different beat each day.

Soon after nine the following morning, fortified by a mighty Highland breakfast in which large slices of Stornoway pudding figured prominently, Jim, Philip and Robbie were on their way to the hill. It was a typical August day for the Hebrides. Overnight rain that had literally hopped off the slates of the hotel roof was in the process of giving way to bright sunshine. Such is the weather in this part of the world. Atlantic depressions sweep in, do their worst, and quickly move on.

Anti-climax is probably the best and most accurate description of the events of the next number of hours. To the educated eye, the heather could not be better suited to the needs of grouse. Rich swathes of young growth liberally topped with purple foliage were intermingled with patches of tall and ancient heather. Grouse would have to be mad to ignore habitat such as this. But this, it seemed, is exactly what they had decided to do. Try as he might, Flint could not locate a single one.

Time passed and the spirits of the sporting trio began to droop. To make matters worse, it had become apparent at an early stage that stopping for the prescribed breather was not a good idea. That most vicious of creatures, the Highland midge, together with its extended family, was only waiting to pounce on hot humanity the moment that it threw itself into the heather.

Around four o'clock the by now thoroughly disgruntled group decided that enough was enough and headed for the car. Trudging back across the heather, Jim's mind was far away when a shout from his son, Robbie, brought him quickly back to reality. Coming straight at him out of the sun and flying only feet above the ground was a big covey of grouse. Or so he thought. As his gun met his shoulder the 'covey' turned at maximum range, giving him little more than a half chance. His single shot found its mark but in the act of firing Jim knew that something was wrong. For a start there were several dozen birds in the 'covey'. And they lacked that plump, rounded shape of your typical grouse. It did not take Flint long to provide Jim with his prize, an out-of-season golden plover.

Back at the hotel the trio's collective humour was not improved when they discovered that they were the only grouseless group. The other beats had not yielded particularly well, no more in fact than threes and fours. But if you hadn't seen a grouse all day...

Relaxing in the bar later that evening the conversation inevitably turned to the next day's sport. Philip, who tended towards the stout side, was secretly dreading the thought of another long and fruitless hike across the heather. The forecast of a real scorcher was not helping matters either. Problem was, however, that he was not prepared to be seen to be wimping out. Jim would never let him live it down. But then, just when it seemed that there was no escape, the Gods decided to smile on him. 'I'm very tired after all that,' announced Robbie, 'I think that I'll settle for a lazy day fishing from the boat.' There were two lochs within the hotel's territory and a boat was available on the bigger one. Jim, meanwhile, was being more than a little bullish about prospects for the morrow. There had to be more grouse out there and he was determined to open his account. Philip saw his opportunity. Compassion personified, he committed himself to an act of true friendship. 'Right,' he said to Jim, 'You bag a few birds and I'll ghillie for Robbie for the day.'

As the weather forecast had promised, Tuesday dawned under a cloudless sky. Jim's allotted beat was the one nearest to the hotel so Philip was able to drop him and Flint off on the way to the loch. It was an easy beat to walk: a long, almost flat moor punctuated at intervals by a number of small hills. At little more than six hundred feet, the first of these was the highest. A well-worn sheep path led up a gentle slope to the top. Following this path, Jim's spirits soared at the sight of a profusion of grouse droppings that littered the bare peat. Clearly there had been a lot of birds in residence in the not-too-distant past. Within minutes Flint provided confirmation. Sixty or so yards ahead, he froze in classical pose in front of a strip of high heather. A gentle nudge with the knee was usually sufficient to urge him forward. Not this time though. Flint was not for moving. The only option therefore was to walk round him and into the high heather.

This simple strategy had the desired effect. With a whirr of wings, a big covey, at least ten strong, was in the air. The nearest bird was no more than ten yards away. Adrenaline inspiring stuff but Jim kept his cool and downed a straightforward right and left. As Flint was collecting the second grouse, Jim noticed that the survivors, which had followed the contour of the hill, were pitching into the heather on the immediate horizon no more than six or seven hundred yards away. These, clearly, were poorly-educated birds that had not been so rudely disturbed before. Resisting the urge to hurry, he made for their point of descent stopping only to whistle up the pointer who was still searching the patch of high heather with a quite extraordinary degree of enthusiasm. Not long afterwards Flint was once more on point. Once again Jim should have taken a pair but it was not to be. Maybe the excitement was too much. The first shot, a comparatively simple one, was well wide of the mark. Disappointment was almost immediately tempered with relief when, quite far out, a grouse collapsed into the heather in response to his second shot.

What happened next should only really happen in the dreams of sportsmen. Four of the covey, having travelled roughly the same distance as before, decided to alight again. This time Flint's services were not required. The grouse, whose education had quite clearly advanced in a very short period, were up and away at Jim's approach. There was only time for a single shot and to his great delight he added a fourth bird to the bag.

By now it was a little after eleven and becoming seriously hot. A short stretch out in the heather would be very welcome but the dreaded midge ordained otherwise. So Jim kept going. 'It can't possibly get any better', he thought to himself. But it did. An hour and a half later his game bag could take no more. Flint had performed with distinction, he had shot well and his bag had risen to nine.

It was clearly time to call a halt to proceedings. The day had exceeded his wildest expectations. The hotel was little more than two miles away and the thought of a long cool drink and a leisurely lunch was becoming compelling.

Around three Jim was dozing in a deck chair in the shade of the hotel's ancient, white gable when a voice brought him back to consciousness. 'You're back early, was it as bad as yesterday?' asked the voice. Opening his eyes, Jim could not help but smile. Standing beside him were his two partners in crime, faces redder than boiled lobsters. Disbelief quickly registered when he recounted the events of the morning. 'I don't believe a word of it,' said the smaller of the two lobsters and set off for the hotel's cold room to confirm his suspicions. Philip, meanwhile, provided Jim with a blow-by-blow account of a rather less than successful day. Literally everything had gone wrong. The boat leaked, a rowlock had broken off and the trout were in anything but an obliging frame of mind. Their efforts, which had been allegedly quite considerable, had been rewarded with a single fish. It was one of those long, extra lean trout of the hill lochs which, on another day, might well have been returned to the water. Worst of all though, because of the stiff breeze out on the loch, they had not realised just how powerful the sun's rays were. Hence the boiled crustacean appearance.

Jim smiled to himself. He would like to have repeated the time-honoured phrase, you win some you lose some. But he was a kind-hearted man and held his peace.

4

One very frosty afternoon

SPELLS OF SERIOUSLY cold weather are rare phenomena in Ireland. Or rather they should be. The Gulf Stream is supposed to see to that. But global warming, if the experts are to be believed, is in the course of changing matters. When the icy winds of winter howl down from the north, that mild lapping current seems to be developing an unfortunate habit of going AWOL. Take 2010 for example. During the latter part of November, and with precious little warning, the mercury suddenly plummeted. By night temperatures dropped to -10°C or lower and by day struggled to get much above freezing. In County Cavan a new record was set in December. During one twenty four hour period the highest temperature recorded was -9.5°C.

Initially that cold snap did wonders for the shooting scene. Teal and woodcock in particular crossed the Irish Sea in droves expecting – poor creatures – to escape the savagery that had descended upon their normal wintering quarters. A clear case of frying pans and fires.

On the third day of the freeze, my youngest son, Paul, rang around noon. He had been up well before dawn, all the tasks on the farm had been completed and he was focussed firmly upon woodcock. He would be over to pick me up, he said, around two.

Bang on the appointed hour, Paul's car pulled into the driveway. As usual, springers Dusty and Misty were yapping furiously in the dog box, impatient to get on with the business in hand. Our destination was Carey's bog. At least that is what I am calling it for the purpose of this narrative. This wet and rushy few acres is surrounded by shallow drains liberally overhung with furze and hazels. On opposite sides it is joined by grassy fields, one narrow, the other large and undulating with damp patches in the hollows. Both fields on their far bounds are bordered by ancient and unkempt blackthorn hedges overhanging partially-blocked drains. These drains are supposed to carry surplus water away from the area but they make an exceptionally poor job of it. At intervals these apologies for drains widen into what may loosely be described as shallow, muddy ponds. If one set out to design winter quarters for woodcock, it would be hard to better Carey's bog and its immediate surrounds.

Then there are the snipe. Not enormous numbers but most days it would be unusual not to flush a dozen or two from the central rushy area. And, just once in a while, the springers are apt to send a cock pheasant hurtling into the air, complaining noisily about the impertinent intrusion into his patch.

Very few shooters know about Carey's bog. And that is just the way we want to keep it. Hence the pseudonym.

A tried and trusted campaign procedure operates for the bog. First we do the outer drains of the adjacent grassy fields. Some six hundred yards away from the bog, the drain of the bigger of the two fields meets a stream. This is the starting point. On the afternoon in question Dusty and Misty were, as usual, quivering in anticipation as they waited to be unleashed. Springers, as aficionados of the breed know only too well, do not hang around. For this reason I take up a position some hundred yards ahead of them and start walking fast. Paul keeps just behind them on the other side. Sometimes the woodcock break the second the dogs get near them and give him some shooting. On other occasions they run, something they are very capable of doing, before getting airborne. These, in theory, are mine.

It was not looking too good until I had nearly reached the bog. Despite the best efforts of the two chocolate and white bundles of energy, not a bird had appeared. Then, at a wide wet patch where hazels abounded, a woodcock broke on the far side. Knowing that Paul was still too far back to take advantage of the situation, I fired at the fast-departing silhouette. It had in fact left my field of view before I pulled the trigger but I knew that I was on target. A mini disaster then ensued. As Paul walked out into the field to pick up the woodcock, a second one emerged and flew off just out of range for him. Worse was to follow. Just as we entered the bog the dogs decided to back-pedal along the drain and, near to where the two birds had emerged, succeeded in flushing a further two. Needless to say both were well out of range.

Next on the agenda was the drain at the far bounds of the second grassy field. As the outer side is a no-go region – the owner prefers to keep it as a game sanctuary – we both have to walk the bog side. There was only one woodcock there and I should have shot it. But I didn't. It came out low only feet ahead of Paul and flew straight towards me. In consequence he could not fire. I should have kept my cool, allowed it to pass and then taken it some thirty yards out. But here theory and practice diverged sharply. As it passed I threw up my gun and fired... at least ten feet behind it I suspect. Sensible bird that it was, it then jigged into the blackthorns and was seen no more.

Some days however the Gods eventually decide to favour one. And this was just one of those days. A couple of hundred yards further on, a single teal rose from a muddy pond which had just sufficient water flowing through it to prevent it from freezing over. As it fell to my shot, six more rose and my second barrel found its mark. These things happen all too quickly in the shooting field but it was not, I suspect, a genuine right and left, as the first teal was almost certainly on the ground before my shot reached the second one. What harm? After an atrocious miss there was nothing wrong with a couple of duck.

Now it was time for the bog itself. At one corner the ground is slightly higher and covered with a dense patch of furze, some quarter of an acre in all. There is usually a better than evens chance of springing a woodcock or two here. A rather circuitous route is necessary to get to the furze without disturbing the snipe. Most times the few shots we fire at woodcock around the edges do not seem to bother them unduly so they can be safely left until last.

Once at the furze, Dusty and Misty hurtled into action. Almost immediately a woodcock broke, giving Paul his first bird of the afternoon. Hardly had the sound of his shot died when two woodcock emerged side by side next to me. That rare possibility of a right and left at these most elusive of birds seemed on but, having downed the first, I could only watch in dismay as the second jinked back into the furze before I could even begin to line it up. Deep inside the cover the two springers could still be heard tearing around with their customary zeal. If nothing else they are a dedicated pair. Despite their best efforts however nothing else emerged.

Now it was time to see if the snipe were in an obliging frame of mind. Keeping the dogs at heel was, as usual, the main problem. Reduced to the passive role of retrieving the slain is not a job spec they are happy with. To be honest more than the odd throaty growl at them is necessary if they are to be prevented from bounding into the rushes.

Some of the wet patches were partly frozen and the snipe were scarcer than usual. Paul, however, distinguished himself by bringing down the three single birds that came his way. I was less lucky. My single long shot failed to find its mark.

By now the sun was just starting to touch the horizon and the cold of a winter's evening was becoming apparent. Those that walk the wild and lonely places will know that special cold all too well. Whilst the sun is still shining, a combination of the faint heat of its rays and internal body heat generated by exercise is just about sufficient to allow one to keep one's mind on the task at hand. But once the sun has left the evening sky, a chill descends that targets fingers, toes and ears. Such was our condition as we left the bog.

The handiest way to exit the place is to crouch low and follow a narrow path through a blackthorn cluster, a path created by generations of cattle seeking better grazing than that on offer in the bog. Still crouching, we were just coming to the end of this path when we were presented with what should have been the icing on the cake. Dusty and Misty, suddenly reinvigorated, threw themselves into a bramble patch causing two fine cock pheasants to explode from it, crowing in indignation. Both should have been bagged. But neither was. Maybe it was the frozen fingertips that tipped the scales in their favour. That was our excuse anyway. The pair of them departed unscathed.

Nothing for it now but to make for the car. We had done something of a circuit and the quickest way was to follow the bank of a small river. Most times it delivers little in the way of game. The gradient is steep causing the flow to be too fast for the likes of mallard and teal. Except in times of heavy frost. Then, with most other waters in the area frozen over, there is always the chance of a visitor or two. And so it proved to be on that frosty evening. We were in sight of the car when a snipe rose from the water's edge. Paul's snap shot brought it tumbling down some thirty yards out on the far side of the river. Problem was though that the springers, questing furiously in and out of the water, had not seen the snipe rise. As a result, in response to the shot they redoubled their efforts along the water's edge. Try as we might we could not persuade them to cross and search for the bird. The only option so was for Paul to make his way back to a farm bridge and do his own retrieving.

There was one last twist to the story. Whilst Paul was backtracking to the bridge I decided that, rather than standing around and getting even colder, a short stroll in the opposite direction might be a better option. And so it proved to be. I was rewarded with a fine duck mallard that the dogs flushed at a point where a tangled mass of vegetation hangs down from the bank.

And that was it. A memorable afternoon with four snipe, three woodcock, two teal and a mallard to show for our efforts. We would visit that special place again next week, we decided. It was not to be however. The weather hardened even more, night temperatures went down to -12°C and a couple of days later a hard weather shooting ban came into operation. Little did Dusty and Misty know, that triumphant evening, that they were in for some three weeks of enforced boredom.

5

The fastest gun alive

MANY SHOOTERS beyond the age of fifty are, at best, half deaf. Not surprising really when one reflects upon the fact that, for a considerable proportion of those fifty years, they have deliberately given rise to enormous decibels in close proximity to their ears. And this to the quite obvious detriment of all those bits and pieces, ear drums, ossicles, fenestrae etc which, poor things, do their level best to get sound waves to the brain. I refer, of course, to those of us whose sport centres around rough shooting and wildfowling. Clay shots and driven shooters, perhaps because they are more sensible, or perhaps because they fire far more cartridges, are much more likely to take sensible precautions to protect their hearing. There is as well the point that for these two groups, covering the ears does not detract from the efficient pursuit of their sport.

In contrast, the wildfowler would be handicapped if he could not hear the whistling of incoming wigeon packs or the noisy clamour of wild geese as they climb from their roosts in the early morning. So too would be the rough shooter if he could not detect that noisy rustle of woodcock tearing from the hazels or the screech of snipe lifting out of rushy tussocks.

These things being said, and despite their (usually) crummy hearing, the great majority of shooters can normally distinguish between two shots, however close together they are fired. In consequence it is quite surprising just how often one fires at a bird, watches it fall and then sees someone else walk over and pick it up or send the dog out to retrieve it. Both parties are entirely convinced that there was a single shot and it was they who fired it. The mathematical chance of two shots being fired at the same precise millisecond should, in theory, be very slim indeed. Yet I find that it happens to me at least once each season.

Back though to the almost instantaneous scenario. Some years back it was sufficient to raise John, a good friend of mine, to near-celebrity status. At the time he and some work colleagues were renting the shooting of nearly two thousand wet and mainly rough acres situated about a mile from the estuary. It was a wonderful place for wildfowl, especially during periods of wild weather when, often starting well before dawn, duck would come streaming in. Geese were not that plentiful in the area but from time to time a few small skeins of pinks were liable to put in an appearance, especially later in the winter.

Many years previously, attempts had been made to reclaim parts of the land but, being exceptionally low lying, they had met with little success. In fact if anything the aborted drainage works had improved the place as far as duck shooting was concerned. Drains which had never been fully dug out held water for much of the year and when the autumn rains came these channels spilled out creating numerous flashes. Rushes grew in profusion on the wet ground and always harboured a few snipe. In places the heaps of clay that had been excavated had provided ideal bases for a number of hides. Now well-colonised with vegetation, they blended splendidly into the background.

For wildfowl however the most attractive feature were two smallish gravel pits that had been dug out during the 1950s. Now exhausted, they had gradually filled with water and were generously fringed with reeds. Tufted duck were nearly always in residence and as autumn progressed they were joined by other divers. Only pochard, inexplicably, were not that plentiful in the area but at times substantial flights of goldeneye were likely to come in at early dawn. These flights were composed almost entirely of ducks. It was a rare and thoroughly unfortunate drake that found its way into the bag.

Very occasionally a handful of Canada geese would come in with the pinks on the morning of a shoot. Why they were not more plentiful is hard to explain. The pits, for all practical purposes, appeared very similar to those that Canadas favour over many parts of southern Britain. It may well have been the absence of islands, a not uncommon feature of gravel pits elsewhere, that was the decisive factor. The resulting lack of secure nesting sites could well have been a deterrent to the colonization of the pits.

When the shoot was first started it was agreed that a member could bring a guest on three mornings each season. There was, however, one stipulation. Only one gun could fire at a time. Initially this was not a problem but, as time went by, the rule gradually became more honoured in its breach than in its observance. Such, it might be observed, is human nature. Eventually it was agreed that something would have to be done. The released mallard, in particular, were especially vulnerable to double broadsides early in the season. Eventually a decision was reached. The guest rule would continue to operate but with one important addition. Only one shotgun could be brought to a hide.

John rarely brought a companion with him on those mornings. This was not, I hasten to add, because there was anything of the pot hunter about him. Rather, it was simply because he was never that comfortable or relaxed when shooting in close proximity to another person. Matters changed though when his eldest son, Chris, entered his early teens. By the time that he had reached his twelfth birthday, Chris had become as addicted to shooting as was his father. And, even at that tender age, he was a more than respectable shot. Whenever opportunity allowed he would accompany his father on shooting expeditions and never missed the three mornings on the duck shoot. John was delighted with the situation, to such an extent that he allowed the young man to do most of the shooting.

There was only one slight problem. Even though Chris was a sturdily-built youngster, his father's magnum twelve was a little on the heavy side for him. At times John could sense his son's frustration when he was unable to shoulder the gun sweetly enough to deal with a fast-crossing tuftie or an incoming teal dropping at knots from the clouds. Because of this John decided to let him bring his twenty bore to the shoots. Conscious of the rules he instilled into his son the fact that they would, strictly, indeed very strictly, shoot only in turn. There would be no double volleys.

This minor transgression benefited Chris enormously and it was not long before his cartridge-to-kill ratio was almost as good as his father's. And, in fairness to him, he stuck religiously to the arrangement whereby he would only take every second shot until, that is, one fateful morning towards the end of the season.

It was one of those days in late January when the weather is neither one thing nor the other. Neither too hot nor too cold, overcast and with little or no wind. In fact the very sort of day upon which fowl feel obliged to fly at heights which challenge even the most expert of shots. John and Chris had had very little shooting all morning and with little more than an hour of the allotted time left, their bag amounted to no more than a couple of wigeon and a teal. John's inclination was to call proceedings to a halt and head for home. But Chris, fuelled by the impetuosity of youth, would have none of this. It could only get better, he argued. Unsurprisingly it did not and the bag remained stubbornly at three.

Then, just when even Chris had to admit it was probably time to go, three mallard appeared flying almost straight towards them: high and handsome as the saying goes. It had been so long since the last shot that neither father nor son could remember whose turn it was. This, however, was to become quickly academic as the mallard, presumably spooked by some slight movement beneath, flared for the heavens.

Forgetting protocol, the two fired almost in unison and, at least forty yards up, two of the mallard folded. Then, realising what they had done, the two could do no more than exchange embarrassed grins. At this stage they were not to know, nor for that matter did it even enter their minds, that the two reports were only just discernable as separate entities.

Our heroes had just got back to the car and stowed their gear when shoot captain Myles Campion, came striding over. Expecting harsh words of reprimand for their disregard of the rules, the duo were more than a little surprised when he called out, 'Well done John, I've never seen anything to equal that. Two birds dead in the air and no more than the tiniest fraction of a second between your shots.' Being an essentially honest man John was about to explain that things were not quite as they may have seemed to be when they were joined by two other members of the syndicate. 'Was that a single trigger gun you were using?' enquired Jim Goodman, 'There's just no way that I could get two shots off that quickly with my old blunderbuss!' 'Brilliant!' said Bob Stokes, 'just brilliant. I always knew that you were a more than handy shot but that exhibition beat all.'

Too late for confession now, John gave Chris the slightest of nudges with his knee. At this point in the proceedings there was little point in giving the game away. The faintest hint of a modest smile crossed John's face. 'A bit of luck really,' he said, 'somehow they just came over perfectly.' Chris, to his eternal credit, just about managed to keep a straight face.

There the matter ended. Or, more correctly, almost ended. At subsequent shoots John tended, once the rising sun lit up the eastern sky, to hold his fire if more than a single high bird passed anywhere near. Reputations, after all, are hard won commodities and, once acquired, need to be guarded jealously.

6

Quite definitely a wild goose chase

WORK, THAT CURSE of the shooting classes, had brought us to this picturesque place, a tiny village nestling in a valley between two small hills. Less than a mile away the Thames meandered through rich farmland, its presence only betrayed by the clusters of pollarded willows that graced its banks.

Our problem, as a family, was finding accommodation for the duration of our stay. Neither the local estate agents, who traded under the magnificent title of Witherspoon, Witherspoon and Halfpenny, nor those in the surrounding villages had been able to come up with anything in the locality. What few lettings there were were for a minimum of one year and we would only be in the area at best for eight or nine months.

It was beginning to look as if we would have to settle for a grim-looking apartment block some twenty miles away when, out of the blue, Witherspoon, Witherspoon and Halfpenny came up with the goods. 'Agnes here from Witherspoons,' said the voice on the phone, 'I think that we've found just what you are looking for. It's an old farmhouse, not in the best of condition but the roof is sound and there is a central heating system of sorts. If you can get here at three this afternoon I'll take you to see it.'

Heavy traffic delayed us on our journey and we were consequently a bit on the late side for our appointment with Agnes. To say that she was a formidable lady would be no understatement. An immaculately groomed and certainly not unattractive person, probably in her late thirties, she was quite clearly not in the business of taking prisoners. 'You're late,' she said, 'and I've got better things to do with my time than hanging around waiting for people.' We later learned that she was *the* Agnes Halfpenny, last of her line and sole proprietor of the outfit. The Witherspoons, in some way distantly related to the Halfpennys, had all long since departed for the great auction rooms in the sky.

The house, though a bit on the ramshackle side, proved to be ideal and, very much to our surprise, the asking rent was less than what we had been expecting. We could move in straightaway and take it on a month–by–month basis. The deal quickly concluded, we were walking back to the cars when a cock pheasant rose at the edge of an unkempt shrubbery and departed crowing in panic. 'Don't shoot, do you?' enquired Agnes. When we told her that we did and, moreover, were quite passionate about it, her next remark stopped us in our tracks. 'Well you can't shoot here,' she said, 'the pheasants are mine.' This, it has to be admitted, was a side of the lady we hadn't exactly expected.

A few days later on a bright Monday morning we moved into the farmhouse. We had barely got ourselves organised when a battered and very muddy four by four squealed to a halt in the yard. Agnes had come to see if everything was OK. She accepted our invitation to stay for a cup of coffee and, as we sat around the ancient oak table in the kitchen, the conversation inevitably turned to shooting. She, it quickly transpired, was as fanatical as we were. Unusually, we learned, there were no serious shoots in the area other than a syndicate headed up by, yes you guessed it, the bold Agnes. It appeared that most of the local farmers allowed her the use of their lands. We suspected that none of them would have the courage to refuse her. 'If you like,' she said, 'you can come and do some vermin shooting with us. We start on the magpies and carrion crows as soon as the nests are completed.'

That spring we joined Agnes and some of her syndicate on a number of evening sorties. These were always conducted with military precision. In the course of her work she kept a careful record of each and every nest as it appeared. Her farmers we discovered were under strict instructions to do likewise. On any one evening a route was worked out which would take in seven or eight nests, sometimes more. At each point of call the strategy was the same. The nest would be surrounded and, if the incubating bird had not already departed, as Agnes approached she would fire a BB into it. Should the bird survive the blast it was usually shot by one of the surrounding guns as it attempted a rapid exit. I don't think that too many were missed. On the one occasion a gun failed to do his duty, a tirade of abuse from the officer commanding was such as to deter any repeat performances of that nature.

After the nesting season we had little contact with Agnes. Just occasionally we would hear of her exploits in the syndicate's pheasant restocking programme. Wild birds were caught up as soon as the shooting season closed and each member of the syndicate had a particular role to play in the breeding and release work. Agnes was responsible for rearing the day old chicks until they reached an age at which they could go outside.

The summer passed and work took up much of our time. We got little shooting except for a couple of days at the pigeons which were attacking the spring wheat on an adjacent holding.

By early autumn our stay in the village was nearing an end and we were in advanced negotiations concerning our next assignment. Towards the end of September we rang Agnes to tell her that we would be moving out at the end of the following month. 'Pity,' was her response, 'we were only saying the other day that we wouldn't mind having you in the syndicate if you were permanent fixtures here. You seem to be made of the right sort of stuff.' High praise indeed. She then went on to ask if we would like to shoot some geese before we left. Never ones to refuse a shooting invitation we indicated that we would very much like to do that.

The geese, it transpired, were Canadas. Between the Thames and a number of flooded gravel pits in the area, there was quite a large and rapidly expanding population. One of Agnes' farmers had, dutifully, reported that they were visiting one of his barley stubbles every morning. They were winging in just after daybreak and over the last week numbers had built up to over one hundred. On hearing the news Agnes had indicated to the farmer that she would leave them for another week or two so that numbers could build up even further. But, much to her amazement, she had been met with a rare display of rank insubordination. 'I'm ploughing the field on Friday,' he told her, 'so if you want a crack at the geese you will have to take it before then.' And he was not, she told me with more than a hint of pique in her voice, for turning.

As a result the shoot was scheduled for the following Thursday morning. We were to meet up in the village outside the White Hart public house forty-five minutes before dawn. We were left to work out for ourselves what time that would actually be. The field in question was no more than ten minutes' drive away but Agnes clearly didn't want any mishaps.

When we reached the rendezvous well before the appointed hour, two members of the syndicate were already there. Despite the fact that Canadas were plentiful in the area this was their first opportunity to have a serious crack at them. They were, in consequence, quite excited about the shoot.

It was a typical October morning, clear and dry with just a hint in the air of the frosts that would soon descend upon the valley. There was little or no breeze but the syndicate members assured us that this would not be a problem. The geese had not been disturbed on the farm and were, according to the farmer, coming in low without bothering to resort to the more customary circuit or two.

Exactly three quarters of an hour before dawn all were present and eager for the off. All that is except Agnes. 'She's hardly ever late,' we were told, 'she'll be along very soon.' But the minutes ticked by and of the lady there was no sign. A sense of restlessness soon started to become apparent amongst the assembled members. We waited and we waited. Then, with ominous streaks of yellow beginning to lighten the eastern sky, the unmistakable sound of a four by four being driven at knots floated across the morning air. 'Blasted brats,' announced Agnes as she hopped out of the vehicle, 'some sort of tummy bug, kept me up half the night.' This was the first time that we became aware of the fact that she was of the married or partnered persuasion. She never wore the customary ring on her left hand. Sometime later that morning I happened to enquire of one of the syndicate members as to what Agnes' man did for a living. 'He's a househusband, poor sod,' was the reply, 'what else could he possibly be?' Sometimes, I suppose, we all ask silly questions.

'We'll have to shift,' shouted the bold Agnes jumping back into her four by four. To say that the convoy hurtled to its destination would be no understatement. Within minutes we were in the farmer's yard and Agnes was busily detailing the battle plan. The geese, apparently, would come in to the stubbles over a low hedge that bounded one side of the field. The field was only one removed from the yard so we would just have time to get down to it and spread out along the hedge, or so we were told. But we hadn't the time. Arriving at the gate of the stubbles it was immediately apparent that we had been beaten to the draw. Well out near the middle of the field, and at least one hundred yards from any boundary ditches, the Canadas were busily hoovering up what was left of the spilled grain.

A council of war was immediately summoned. 'Only one thing for it now,' said the commander in chief, 'if we work it properly they will more or less certainly go out the way they came in.' So half of us were despatched by an extremely circuitous route to the far side of the hedge and the remainder, who might be loosely thought of as walking guns, set out for strategic points around the field boundary.

As soon as those who were crouched in ambush behind the hedge were in position the walking guns hopped over the ditches into the stubbles. Then, as they advanced, a sea of heads shot up as the Canadas, unused to such rude intrusion, began to engage in a serious bout of 'ker–honking.' At this the advancing guns broke into a run in the hope of getting a shot before the geese departed the place. They were out of luck. As too were those concealed behind the hedge. In response to the rapid advance of humanity the geese rose *en masse*, quickly gained height and exited the field in all directions. A few long and extremely hopeful shots failed to dislodge as much as a single feather. And then they were gone.

Shortly afterwards a thoroughly disconsolate band of shooters met up in the yard. Only one comment was made. And yes, it was by Agnes. 'If you'd run a bit faster you might have got a few,' she snapped before getting into the four by four and departing in a cloud of dust.

Nothing more to report.

That was the last we ever saw of the lady.

7

A first encounter

IN TERMS OF the shooting calendar the first couple of weeks of October can be something of a slack period in Ireland. The grouse season is over for the year and pheasant and woodcock can sleep easy until the first of November. Woodcock, anyway, are not yet that plentiful. It is reckoned that no more than ten per cent of the mid-winter population consists of home-bred birds. The great flood of winter visitors from Scandinavia and the Baltic States does not really gain momentum until around the time of the November full moon. Even the duck are rather less than obliging. Those mallard fortunate enough to survive the early season barrages are now all too well aware of the evil designs of mankind and tend to keep a respectful distance.

As to the migrants, the big annual influx of teal and wigeon, and for that matter snipe, is now only getting underway and it will be a while yet before they are here in serious numbers.

All this means that we have to dream of the good times to come and content ourselves with the occasional evening flight or a leisurely stroll across the bogs or along the river bank. And, for the latter enterprise, the earlier in the morning the better. Mallard in particular do not hang around for too long in their nocturnal haunts once the world awakes from slumber.

It was on one such morning during October in the early 1970s that two of my sons and I decided to try a small river not too far from the house. River, perhaps, is something of an exaggeration. Stream would be a more accurate description. In those days it was a wonderful place for wildfowl, especially later in the winter. Running through a rugged valley known locally as the Skibereen, it alternated between short, fast flowing stretches and marshy patches where the water spilled out into rush-covered hollows every time there was heavy rain. During periods of severe frost it was really at its best. When everywhere else in the locality was frozen, teal would pour in as dusk descended. Indeed there were evenings when the flight got underway before a scarlet sun had slipped fully beneath the horizon. In my mind's eye I can still see the first packs of small black silhouettes coming in from the west against the background of the setting sun.

Today alas the Skibereen is a very different place. A few years back all manner of heavy machinery moved in, the furze was torn from the steep slopes on either side and the bed of the stream was lowered some five or six feet. In terms of duck habitat it is now little more than a shadow of its former self. Progress, I am told, is what it is called.

The name Skibereen had, incidentally, long puzzled me. Most present day Irish place names are anglicisations of the original Gaelic name which, not infrequently, accurately described the nature of the surroundings. But my problem was that our Skibereen could not bear less resemblance to the lovely small town and fishing port of the same name in west Cork. Then, last summer all was finally revealed. By great good fortune I happened to be walking the bank of the stream one evening when I met a very old man who was originally from the area. Now living in Dublin he was back visiting a son who resided in the neighbourhood. The old man turned out to be no mean Gaelic scholar and it took him no time at all to explain the apparent contradiction. Skibereen (the town) derived its name from the Gaelic word *Sciobhairin*, literally and most appropriately the place of the little boats.

Our Skibereen, in contrast, had come from *Scibirlin* meaning, again appropriately, a poor patch of land. Most unusually, two words with very different meanings had been, over the centuries, corrupted into one.

The handiest way to get to the Skibereen is to drive down a long lane which comes to an end only two fields away. This brings one to a point almost midway between a wet, spring-fed area where the stream rises and its end where it enters the river Suir. In those days the normal form was for me to take off downstream whilst the lads took the opposite direction. They were young at the time and always eager for the fray. No sooner were we at the bank of the stream that morning than they were gone. I was about to set off when, towards the edge of a rough pasture across the stream, a strange moving object caught my attention. What I can only describe as a black and grey-brown football was rolling around in the grass emitting high-pitched screams. Intrigued by this extraordinary vision I walked down to the water's edge to get a better view.

I was little more than twenty yards away when the black component of the football detached itself and ran towards the remains of a fallen elm. Although I had never seen one before, there was little doubt but that this largish stoat–like creature was a mink. It had clearly become aware of my presence and let go of the rabbit which formed the other half of the football. The said rabbit was left lying on its side. It was motionless and looked extremely dead.

Whilst we were well aware of the spread of mink in the UK and the depredations of which they were capable, we gave them little thought here in Ireland at the time. Little did we realise in the early 1970s how quickly that particular plague was going to hit us. The problem had its origins some fifteen years earlier when small farmers, especially in the Border counties, were advised by officialdom that mink could provide them with a reasonable living on just a few acres. What officialdom failed to tell them was that mink eat an awful lot of expensive meat and are slow to provide a return on one's investment. The result was quite predictable. Some of the farmers, unwilling to put up with lodgers who were not paying their way, simply opened their gates and ordered them out. On top of this, other mink began to escape from the farms which had endeavoured to soldier on. Events in the UK were being paralleled in Ireland. Waterway after waterway was colonized as a feral population started to expand and spread to the west and to the south. My first sighting on that October morning in the Skibereen was at least one hundred miles from the nearest mink farm.

Hoping that the mink would make a reappearance and give me the chance of a shot I crouched down on one knee and awaited events. The dead elm had clearly fallen a good number of years earlier and several rabbit burrows were evident beneath it. It was into one of these burrows that the mink had retreated. I did not have too long to wait. A flash of black at the entrance to the burrow indicated that the mink's blood-lust was up and it wanted to continue the business of securing its dinner. Before I could raise the gun it literally hurtled across the grass and re-engaged with the rabbit. To my amazement the rabbit was anything but dead and started to scream again as its oppressor pounced. The reconstructed football immediately began to roll around the field as before. Then, for no apparent reason, the mink detached itself again and ran to the safety of the burrow. I could only assume that, despite my stillness, it was less than happy about my presence.

Anyway, this time it was rather more reluctant to leave its sanctuary. On a couple of occasions the tip of its nose appeared only to be withdrawn at speed. Meanwhile the rabbit lay motionless only a few yards away.

Eventually though, aggression got the better of it once again and like a flash it was out and pouncing on the unfortunate rabbit. And again the screaming started. It was now quite clear that I was not going to get a clean shot at the mink. Its bolt hole was simply much too near the rabbit. Nothing for it therefore but to fire at the football – after all, it seemed unlikely that the rabbit was going to last much longer.

What happened at this juncture was not quite what I expected. At my shot the football fell apart and, unbelievably, the rabbit took off across the field. So much for the conventional 'wisdom' about the single fatal bite to the back of the head or in the throat about which I had read so much. Just how that rabbit was able to withstand a number of near-death experiences and then a charge of No 7 shot is beyond explanation. I have often wondered if it survived for long. All I can say is that, if it did, it certainly had the right genes to father or mother a large number of genuine survivors. As to the mink, it was as dead as the proverbial maggot. In the fullness of time it was despatched to a taxidermist in Kilkenny and now occupies a position of honour on top of the fishing tackle cabinet in my study.

There is only one thing to add about that morning. Not long after I had retrieved the dead mink, the boys appeared with a couple of mallard and three teal. They had never been much more than half a mile from me, yet so engrossed was I watching the unfolding drama, I did not hear so much as a single shot.

8

A problem solved

MURTAGH'S FARM had been acquired by Simon's grandfather after the end of the First World War. And Old Tom, as he was universally known, had worked hard and long to develop the sixteen hundred or so mixed Norfolk acres into the fine holding that it now undoubtedly was. Well over half the farm had always been top class land which, year after year, produced high yielding crops of barley and sugar beet. Most of the rest was on the heavy side despite a drainage system that could be traced back to the middle of the 19th Century. Gradually, as cash allowed, and cash was something of a scarce commodity in that part of rural England in the 1920s and 1930s, Old Tom had religiously widened and deepened existing drains and dug out new ones where the original system was failing to deliver.

By the time that Simon's father had taken over the reins in the 1960s well over ninety per cent of the land was subject to an intensive tillage regime. Much of what was left, some half dozen patches varying in size between two and ten acres, had been abandoned to its own devices. The cost of reclamation would have been just too high and, anyway, there was no guarantee that the final product would ever amount to much more than middling ground.

Strangely, in a part of the country in which there had long been a strong game shooting tradition, neither Simon's father or grandfather had any real interest in the sport. There were shotguns in the house, four in fact, standing in a gleaming row in the glass-fronted mahogany cabinet in the study. But what action they saw rarely amounted to much more than the annual series of skirmishes with rooks and wood pigeons as the harvest ripened. At least that was the situation until Simon entered his teens.

It had been the tussles with the grey hordes that gave the young man his first taste of shooting, a taste that quickly developed into a passion. From the time the first hint of yellow appeared in the winter barley, his summer days were devoted to the pursuit of pigeons. Then there were the partridges. Real grey ones, not your Johnny-come-lately red-legs. Though not nearly as plentiful as in former times, there was still sufficient of them to meet the needs of the youthful gunner and his friends. September 1st was the most eagerly awaited day on the calendar. Soon after dawn the young men would be found out in the golden stubbles, rather higher than is now the case, tense with anticipation of that rush of wings as the first covey took to the air. They would not hunt the beet until later in the morning. Experience had taught them that the partridges were never greatly enamoured with the crop, probably because it was just too dense to allow them much freedom of movement. It was really a place of last resort when they had been subjected to serious disturbance.

Sometimes the survivors of a covey would seek refuge in the luxuriant rough growth that sprouted in the abandoned low lying parts of the farm. When the dogs were sent in to locate them they almost invariably disturbed a few duck. Left to nature these hollows had become, effectively, a series of mini wetlands. Even in mid summer there were usually pools of water present and these attracted quite substantial numbers of mallard. They were wont to spend their days lazing on the water and, once the harvest had been saved, would flight back and forth to the stubbles. Perhaps surprisingly, considering Simon's passion for shooting, they were only rarely fired upon. There was usually a simple explanation for this. Like as not, partridge and duck would be in the air together and, under such circumstances, there was no doubt as to who would play second fiddle.

Early in the 1970s two events occurred which would have a profound effect upon Simon's shooting career. First there was the rapid and serious decline in the partridge population. In the course of a very short number of years the dozen or so coveys that he would expect to meet on opening day dwindled away to no more than two or three. Why this happened he was at a total loss to explain. Nothing had really changed on the farm either in terms of habitat or agricultural activity. And, most certainly, they had not shot the partridges more heavily than in former years.

The second event was the arrival at the farm of a new manager, or more correctly in the context of this narrative, of his son. About the same age as Simon, Will was also a fanatical shooter. But from a very different background. He had grown up many miles away in the north west. And, whilst Simon's passion had been fuelled by pigeons and partridges, Will's love of shooting had its origins on salt marsh and estuary and the wigeon and pintail hordes that made these places their home.

Not surprisingly the two quickly became firm friends. Initially Will had been rather less than enthusiastic about the prospect of moving inland and miles away from his wildfowling haunts. But once he had found the wet places on the farm and realised their potential, he was a man transformed. Especially when he discovered that, in addition to the local mallard, significant numbers of migratory fowl frequented the area during the autumn and winter months.

It was Will who, one winter's evening, threw out the suggestion that was to plot the course of future events on the farm in so far as shooting was concerned. 'Why don't you form a syndicate for the duck shooting?' he enquired of Simon. 'Properly run, we could have some great sport,' he continued, 'and as well as that, you could make a handy few bob.'

Maybe it was Will's infectious enthusiasm, or maybe it was the demise of the partridge shooting or, most likely, a combination of the two that set Simon thinking. Since Will's arrival he had spent quite a lot of time flighting the various pools and flashes on the farm and developed something of a liking for it. His father had no objection, indeed he took the view that anything which added to the farm's cash flow would be more than welcome. And so the syndicate was born.

Will had already nailed his colours to the mast. 'Look,' he said to Simon, 'I can't afford a gun like the wealthy b★★★★★★s you will be getting but I'll make you a deal. Give me a gun in the syndicate and I'll do all the necessary work. Rearing, releasing, feeding, you name it and I'll do it.' Simon, now becoming more and more involved in the day-to-day running of the farm, was more than happy to agree to the proposition.

The shoot could have developed purely as a wild bird one. Between the resident mallard and winter migrants there was no shortage of duck and a sensible feeding programme would have attracted more than adequate numbers on shoot mornings. But neither Simon nor Will were men who liked doing things in half measures. From the start it was decided to release substantial numbers of young mallard in late June.

From the outset the shoot was a great success. Shooting took place on alternate Saturday mornings from pre-dawn greyness to noon. There was rarely a poor day. Rules for the syndicate were simple, in fact there were only three: one gun per hide, all birds to be brought to the barn adjacent to Simon's house at the end of the morning and, in the case of mallard, a bag limit of eight.

The years passed and the syndicate membership remained intact. Indeed it became more and more like a family shoot. One problem, however, began to emerge. Not a major one I hasten to add, but one which was beginning to impinge upon the otherwise harmonious relationships that had developed. One of the members, Mike Cowen, a genuinely popular member, had what in charity might be described as a weakness. He could not, or would not, adhere to the bag limit. At the post-shoot count he would almost invariably arrive with a 'surplus' of mallard. One day he might have nine or ten, another day a dozen. Initially the matter was not an issue, no one was going to get excited about an extra bird or two. And anyway, being something of a rogue, Mike always had a plausible explanation. 'I was just leaving when I noticed a couple of wounded birds in the reeds,' was one such. 'On the way back the dog picked up a few birds. I don't know who shot them,' was another. And, 'I was certain it was a pochard coming straight at me,' was yet another.

Now any sensible man, one might think, would have realised that to everything there is a limit and that his colleagues were unlikely to be overjoyed with the situation. But not Mike.

It was on a Saturday during the Christmas period that matters finally came to a head. A blustery wind had kept the birds low and shooting had been brisk for much of the morning. At the count all the members were in high spirits and enjoying rather more than one convivial drink to celebrate the festive season. All the members that is bar one. Of Mike there was no sign. Curious to know why, everyone stayed on a bit longer than usual.

A considerable amount of time was to pass before their curiosity was satisfied. Eventually all was revealed when what could only be described as an apparition entered the barn. The apparition was just about recognisable as Mike. Just about, because his body was almost totally obscured by duck. There were strings of mallard around his shoulders and hanging from his waist. In fact only his head could be considered to be a mallard free–zone.

Circumstances clearly demanded an explanation. Unhesitatingly Mike obliged. With all the panache of a seasoned warrior he rounded on his colleagues and posed *the* question. 'What sort of useless dogs have you all got?' he demanded to know, 'I've spent the last hour and a half picking up duck everywhere. Wounded ones, dead ones, it was nothing short of a disgrace to leave so many lying around'. A clear case of game, set and match. No one present on that fateful morning was able to nail the miscreant.

That, though, was far from the end of the matter. Later that evening Simon and Will put their heads together. The easy option would have been to politely suggest to Mike that he make alterna-tive shooting arrangements for the following season. But that was not something they were inclined to do. Despite everything they had a sneaking regard for the man. Accordingly an alternative strategy was required. But what?

A chance comment by Simon eventually provided the way forward. 'If he's so bloody keen on retrieving maybe we should pay him to do the job,' he suggested, more in frustration than anything else. He did not exactly expect Will's reply. 'You've got it,' he said, 'or at least very nearly. This is what we'll do.' Over the next few days a number of discreet phone calls were made and all the recipients were pledged to secrecy.

Conditions at the next shoot were not ideal. It had rained steadily throughout the night and squally showers were still flying as the guns set out for their allotted hides in that special blackness that precedes the dawn. But if it was a rather less than ideal morning for duck shooting, the same could not be said for the conspiracy that was about to unfold. All-important, the fact was obscured, at least from Mike, that he was the only one present with dogs in tow. It would be some time before he became aware of this.

As is so often the case on a wet morning, the shooting was slow and very few birds were shot during the first hour.

The morning was well advanced before a clearance came in from the west. Time now for Will to advance the strategy. He made his way over to Mike's hide. 'Sorry to bother you,' he said, 'but I could do with a bit of help. There's a wounder flapping around out in front of my hide and Jake, blast him, has gone AWOL.' Mike obliged but unsurprisingly could not locate the duck. He had barely returned to his hide when his mobile rang. Will, profoundly apologetic, needed his help again. Another member of the syndicate, Andy Kerr, was in trouble. His dog too had gone AWOL and he had a number of birds to be picked. In fairness to Mike he set off again without a murmur to assist his colleague.

And so the scene was set for the rest of the morning. Only the excuses for requiring Mike's assistance were different. Mike, and more specifically his two black Labradors, found themselves the subject of near universal demand. Hardly had he responded to one request than his phone was ringing again. Intelligent man that he was, it did not take him too long to put the proverbial two and two together. He could have switched off his phone and got on with his shooting. But he didn't. An essentially decent man, he responded to every call with just a suspicion of a smile on his face.

When the team met up after the shoot, all were profuse in their thanks for Mike's assistance and, of course, most apologetic for interrupting his sport. Dogs, or rather the lack of them, were not mentioned.

And that, basically was that. The message clearly got through. The following season, Mike never once 'miscalculated' his bag. As Simon remarked to Will in the words of a long-running TV serial, 'It's great when a plan comes together.'

9

Arrival of the duck

TO THOSE WHO love wild and lonesome places, the very phrase 'arrival of the duck' will surely conjure up some predictable images. In the mind's eye they will see wind-swept sea lochs, dark estuaries and packs of black silhouettes dropping fast from leaden skies. They will think too of those same black silhouettes rising from distant and far-flung breeding grounds to begin the annual trek south. And they will hear sounds that they have not heard for many months. There will be the rush of wings and the whistling of wigeon packs. There will be the high pitched piping of teal. And, like as not, in the background they will hear that magic music of the wild geese.

This story however is not about migration. Not, at least, in the conventional sense. The duck that we are about to meet will indeed be going to their wintering grounds, but they will not be taking the usual aerial route. Instead they will travel by road in the dubious comfort of yellow plastic crates. It will be a relatively short journey for them and, unlike the journeys undertaken by their wild brethren, it will require absolutely no energy expenditure on their part.

But I must start at the beginning. We are fortunate in that we have a number of flight ponds on the farm. The biggest of these, roughly circular, and some eighty yards in diameter, serves also as the focus for our annual release programme. In its centre is a large, flat island on which the duck are encouraged to feed and on which, it is always our fervent hope, they will while away the hours preening and sleeping. Because of the security provided by the island we do not bother with the niceties of a release pen. Constant encouragement, in the form of copious quantities of barley, to treat the island as their home is usually sufficient to keep the new arrivals where we want them.

Before the big day, which is usually around the 1st July, there are two matters that require our attention. The first of these is to make as big a dent as possible in the local population of four-legged predators. A quick check around the pond is likely to reveal a few fox scats, like as not produced by a three-quarters-grown cub who could take a serious toll of naïve young mallard. The fox trap is therefore brought into play. It is set up on a well-used path in early June. Most years we pick up two or three at this stage.

Then there are the mink. With the river less than a mile away, they are always a potential threat. We can almost guarantee that they will pay a visit at some stage. The moorhens are a useful indicator during the summer month. If they are on the pond in June, most likely engaged in producing a second brood, all is well. Slow by comparison to other waterfowl they are the first to disappear when mink move in.

To be on the safe side a cage trap is set up on the bank of a nearby stream which leads to the river. This is their usual route to the pond. Star-shaped tracks in a muddy patch indicate where they come ashore. This is the spot at which, well camouflaged, the trap is set. In June there is always a good chance that the mother will have her young in tow, in which case it is possible, with a little luck, to capture the entire family over a period of a few days.

The second task is to strim sections of the island, especially over the front section which is used for feeding in the early days. By late March, much of the island is an emerald jungle, far greener than any field on the farm. This is because last year's birds left behind a rich supply of nitrogen in their droppings. Come the latter days of June the place has every appearance of a hay meadow of long ago and requires a couple of hours of strenuous work with the strimmer to lick it into shape. Patches of high vegetation are always left, in particular under the willow and alder trees which were planted on the island. These patches are essential for the casualties which will inevitably occur in the weeks ahead. Bullying is always a minor problem and the victims must have places where they can hide from their oppressors if they are to have any chance of survival. Lameness is another problem. I have never been able to explain why it occurs but most days at feeding time one or two ducks come hobbling out of the cover. Usually they are back to form after a couple of days. Rest in a secure and undisturbed spot seems to be the answer.

On the appointed day our mallard will not be travelling for long as by great good fortune the game farm is only a little over seven miles away. Martin, the proprietor, will be up at dawn catching up and crating our consignment ...... three hundred in all. We have the option of taking four and a half or six week olds. Our preference is always for the latter. Since we don't use a release pen we reckon that the slightly older birds are just that little bit better when it comes to coping with new surroundings.

There is just one last job to do before they arrive. The strimmed area on the front of the island must be liberally laced with a mixture of pelleted food and barley. Up until now the young duck have been used to an almost exclusive diet of pellets. It is our intention to wean them off these and onto more natural foods as quickly as possible. Hence barley from day one. As the days pass we then gradually reduce the proportion of pellets in the mix. We broadcast the food over a fairly wide area in the hope of persuading our guests to treat the place as a home from home. Later, when they become too adept at finding the food in the short grass, we spread it through the heavier stuff as well. The more time that they spend on the island, the better their survival chances until they come to terms with the ways of a wicked world!

Now it's time for some hard work. The ground in the vicinity of the pond is far too rough to allow the truck and trailer to make a close approach. No option so but to carry the crates over the better part of a hundred yards to the edge of the pond. Hard work? Try it sometime and decide for yourself. Arms outstretched, a dozen or so plump young duck plus a crate weighing one down and a precarious pathway to be negotiated. And to make matters worse, with the crate jutting out in front it is impossible to see where one is putting one's foot down. If you did this a few times a day it would not be long until you were as fit as the proverbial fiddle.

The next half hour is sure to provide some fascinating entertainment. As soon as the sliding door of the crate is pulled back at the edge of the pond, the occupants make a dive for freedom. Except for the odd one which, partly traumatised by the pace of changing events, is likely to cower at the back of the crate. It shouldn't be too difficult to persuade it to join its colleagues.

Contact with water, lots of it, has a profound effect upon the young duck. Until this moment, contact has been pretty minimal. The game farm cannot be blamed for this. There is no way that they could provide adequately for the tens of thousands of birds that pass through the premises each summer.

Delighted to have finally reached what is effectively their natural environment, the releasees immediately start to engage in a bout of frenzied activity. Some skitter across the water surface. Others dive, resurface and dive again. Yet others rise up on their paddles and furiously flap their still tiny wings. In minutes the pond becomes a stage for some great pantomime in which countless acts are performed simultaneously. Insects are snapped from the air and from the water, ducks zigzag in and out of reed beds as they explore their new home. Now and again they pause for a drink.

Next on the agenda is a prolonged spell of preening. Contact with all this water triggers an ancestral reflex which ensures that feathers are properly oiled and tended. The duck use their bills to pull on the stumpy oil gland above their tails and set it secreting. Some do their preening, initially at least, on water. Most however make for the gently-sloping banks of the island. As a general rule it seems that the gymnastics associated with preening are better carried out on *terra firma*.

Mallard minds can now be expected to turn to thoughts of food. At this stage there is so much scattered around that even the most myopic cannot fail to find sufficient. Chattering contentedly, they rush around gorging themselves with all the good things on offer. Then, gradually, activity begins to subside and the majority pause for a rest. Standing in massed ranks they give every appearance of a small army. A few, still exhilarated by their new-found freedom, continue to hop in and out of the water. But they will soon tire and join their comrades. For the time being they are safe and we can steal away. But first one simple precaution before we go. Chances are a young fox may have become aware of unusual happenings on his patch. He might just decide on a visit and could all too easily pick off an unwary young duck which had the bad sense to stray too near the edge. This is why we brought some old and recently worn clothes with us. Left hanging on posts near the pond they may dissuade Reynard from paying too close a call.

Early afternoon now and time for a quick check. One can never be too careful, especially during the first few days. We haven't seen any sparrowhawks or peregrines around for a while but they have an uncanny knack of turning up when least expected. Both are more than capable of taking a serious toll of young duck. Down the years hen sparrowhawks in particular have provided us with our fair share of problems. Today though all seems well. The new arrivals are scattered across the pond and the island. Some are preening again, others back on the food trail. One or two are still darting around exploring their new domain. With reasonable confidence we can leave them to their own devices until the late evening.

And so to the final visit of the day. The game plan is quite straightforward. About an hour before dusk wade out to the island and once again distribute copious amounts of food. Initially the duck are nervous when we splash across and they keep a respectful distance. But food is too attractive a proposition and it does not take them long to decide that this new humanity can be ignored safely. There is a good reason for feeding them at this hour. Their food is on the dry side and once crops are well stuffed they return to water for a drink. Herein lies a problem. They tend to dally on the water so it makes good sense to engineer a reasonable amount of time to get this particular period out of the way before nightfall. Hopefully they will tire of the water and return to the sanctuary of the island before darkness finally descends. The inevitable few, of course, will remain swimming around and at times get dangerously near the bank. Not a lot that we can do about this. If they persist with such cavalier behaviour they may not survive to enjoy our hospitality for long. The bank at night is a dangerous place for innocents.

As we depart we have a final task. Retreating a reasonable distance from the pond so as not to cause consternation to our new guests, we fire a few shots into the evening sky. This is the hour when adult foxes emerge from the den and a little disturbance may, just may, cause them to plan a different route for their nocturnal journeys of pillage. Wishful thinking some might feel, but over the years it has become part of the routine.

At last that long first day has wound to a close. In fairness we have done all in our power to ensure the wellbeing of our charges. In the weeks to come there will be countless more visits to the pond. Such diligence, if there is any fairness in life, should reap handsome dividends. Come autumn all but a tardy few of the mallard will be flying strongly, luring in their wild cousins and guaranteeing us sport in the weeks and months ahead.

10

A morning with a difference

LIKE HIS FATHER and grandfather before him Tim was an avid punt gunner. In fact, since taking off on his first solo outing on the estuary at the tender age of fifteen it would be no exaggeration to say that he had become totally addicted to the sport. September could never come quickly enough for him. Whilst others would be enjoying the balmy days of summer, there was always something of a restlessness about Tim at this time of year. Blue waters with the sun sparkling on the waves were not his idea of what the sea was all about. He craved for the grey mornings of autumn, the lonely estuary and the myriad calls of wildfowl and waders that came with each breaking dawn.

Grandfather Mike had built the punt himself forty years earlier. Grey-green and elegant it bore every sign of careful maintenance. Perfectly balanced, something vital for a craft that rode so low in the water, it was equally manoeuvrable with pole or paddles.

By comparison to his father and grandfather there was one difference in the way that Tim went about his business. Behind the house, a short cobbled path led down to the boathouse in which the punt was berthed. In their day it was only a matter of gathering up gun and cripple stopper and, within minutes, pushing out across the water in search of wildfowl packs. Indeed it was not inconceivable that a shot might present itself within half an hour or so. But times had changed. And changed quite drastically. In only a few short years the level of activity on the estuary had increased alarmingly, changed to such an extent that, more and more, the wigeon packs were tending to give the immediate area a wide berth. Even the mallard, a slightly more trusting species, now rarely put in an appearance other than in ones and twos. First it had been the fish farm: a double row of great cages was anchored almost straight across from the boat house. Every year the row seemed to get longer and, always, boats were passing to and from the cages. Then it was the sailing boats. Years ago it was only the very odd one that ventured this far down the estuary. Now they were coming in ever-increasing numbers into what Tim liked to think of as 'his' waters. Even on the coldest of winter mornings there would be, like as not, a couple of boats out on the estuary.

So Tim was forced to travel some three miles down towards the sea in order to meet up with the fowl. Not only was this enormously time-consuming, it was also extremely hard work, especially when faced with a rising tide. There was only one solution he had decided. He acquired a sixteen-foot boat of ancient but rather more than solid construction. It came complete with outboard. With the punt in tow he could now reach his fowling waters in reasonable time.

Whenever possible it was his practice to set out from the boat-house forty minutes before dawn. His first port of call was an area of mussel beds which formed a sheltered lagoon. The water here was usually quite shallow so he could anchor the boat and wade over to the punt. All going well, it took only a matter of minutes to transfer the guns and other gear to the punt. He could then be out on the estuary in the half light.

There was only one minor drawback to this rather novel way of embarking on a punting expedition. The boat, being of ultra-solid construction, was apt to give him a false impression of the state of the water. A stiff breeze of, for example, around force three could go all but unnoticed by an occupant of the boat. It was not until he had transferred to the punt that Tim would really know whether or not the forthcoming trip was likely to be on the rough side. This however was something that went with the territory and rarely gave him much cause for concern. Until, that is, one fateful morning which he was never destined to forget.

That year the duck had been late coming to the estuary. Despite a couple of minor storms which, according to the weather experts, were remnants of Caribbean hurricanes, November was well advanced before serious packs began to put in an appearance. But even when they did arrive Tim had very little luck. For most of the month the water had been on the choppy side and the wigeon, for new arrivals, were that bit jumpy. He had yet to pull off what might be described as a half decent shot.

It was not until the last Saturday of the month that he felt any real cause for optimism. From the upstairs windows at the front of the house there was a panoramic view of the estuary stretching all the way down to the sea. In the early afternoon he noticed sizeable packs of duck on the move. Flying high they were all following roughly the same pathway. Each pack in turn came up the estuary only to turn some distance above the house and head back in the direction of his fowling grounds. Most of them were wigeon. There were also scaup on the move. These, as is their wont, were flying low, barely skimming the waves. The appearance of scaup was unusual as they were duck that rarely used the estuary. Most years it would take a storm of really ferocious proportions to make them venture in from the sea. Tim's father and grandfather had both hunted scaup and always spoke in the most complimentary of terms about their performance on the dinner table. He had tasted them himself once. And once, he reckoned, was more than enough. As far as Tim was concerned their flesh was tough, oily and anything but palatable. In consequence it had not worried him a jot when scaup were removed from the quarry list a few years previously.

The following morning Tim was up and out well before dawn. The prospect of a positive meeting with the wigeon had kept him awake half the night. As he eased the boat out of the boathouse with the punt in tow he became conscious of an almost eerie stillness.

There was not a breath of wind and not so much as a ripple on the water. Although it was still quite dark, the inhabitants of the estuary were already beginning to welcome a new day. The 'curlee' of the curlews on the mud banks and the high pitched 'klee-ee' of oyster-catchers were part of that familiar orchestra. As he made his way down the estuary, an occasional rush of wings indicated the passing of a wader flock. Godwits perhaps, or even the much smaller knot, it was just too dark to make them out.

Arriving at the mussel beds, Tim was a shade lucky to be able to reach the spot at which he usually put down the anchor. The tide was well out and the water in the lagoon little more than a foot in depth. Quickly he transferred his gear to the punt. Not too distant wigeon cocks were beginning to advertise their presence and he was eager to be off. Perhaps because of this eagerness it did not dawn on him how strange the stillness of the morning really was. It was not the stillness of those icy dawns when all feeling deserts the fingers and toes and breath becomes a white cloud in front of one's face. No, this was that sort of enforced stillness and silence one sometimes gets at a rugby international as the kicker lines up for a shot at goal.

Out on the open water Tim set his course for a shallow bay much favoured by dabbling duck. Wigeon were rarely absent. Teal likewise. And, more often than not, a few pintail and shoveler would grace the place with their presence. The light was now coming and, nearing his destination, he could just make out a large assembly of fowl very near to the shore. Some were up on the mud. There was, however, one problem. This particular bay was peppered with rocks. When the tide was full it was possible to glide in over them. But at this stage of the tide, many rocks were breaking the surface. Negotiating a route that might get him into range was going to be difficult. It was however an opportunity that he was unwilling to miss out on so he decided to give it a try. Painfully slowly he propelled the punt through the rocks. The submerged ones were the real problem. Even at the slowest rate of progress any of them could tear the bottom out of the punt. A full ten minutes passed before realisation finally dawned. Despite his best efforts he was still nearly two hundred yards away from the duck and was unlikely to be able to get much closer.

A disappointed Tim was about to turn the punt when fate took a hand. A sudden and totally unexpected gust of wind suddenly swung the punt to one side and, out of the corner of his eye, he spotted a number of tightly packed objects way out in open water. By their size they were more or less certainly mallard. Elated at this stroke of good fortune, he failed to notice an ominous bank of grey black cloud building in the far south west.

Carefully easing the punt away from the last of the rocks Tim set out in pursuit of the mallard. It was only then, as he moved out into the open channel, that he became aware that the weather was beginning to deteriorate. The wind was gusting with increasing frequency though, at this point, it was not of a strength that might cause him to abandon the attempt. It was simply making his approach a lot more difficult. Steadily he closed in on the bobbing cluster of silhouettes.

For reasons best known to themselves, the mallard seemed disinclined to take any notice of the approaching punt. Slightly less than ninety yards out Tim decided to take his shot. He was long enough at the job to know that the sleepiest-looking body of fowl could, without warning, lift and be gone. As was his custom he slapped the side of the punt with his left paddle an instant before discharging the gun. The shot charge found its mark and eight mallard lay dead on the water. A further three were making every effort to swim away as quickly as possible. The nearest of these he was able to despatch with the cripple stopper. But then, at the shot, the two survivors managed to struggle into the air, only for one of them to almost immediately fall back into the water. Again the cripple stopper did its job. The last survivor, having flown several hundred yards, pitched down and began swimming away furiously once more. Tim quickly gathered up the slain and set out in pursuit of this last bird.

The subsequent chase took him well out into the estuary. The mallard, swimming strongly, had clearly no intention of surrendering.

On several occasions it dived only to resurface in a different quarter. Meanwhile the cloud cover had built up with alarming suddenness. Heavy drops of rain began to fall. The wind, now that bit stronger, was making navigation difficult. Several minutes passed before he was able to finally despatch the duck and turn for home. The journey that lay ahead, he knew, was going to be a hard one.

Rarely had he seen conditions on the estuary go downhill so quickly. Ominous and disturbing thoughts concerning mortality began to filter through Tim's mind. In retrospect, he realised, the pursuit of that final mallard, humane as it was, was little short of foolhardy. 'Keep cool', he whispered to himself, 'and paddle like hell.' Now few would accuse him of being a religious man but, at this juncture, more than a single prayer passed his lips. Buffeted by the wind and shipping water with each breaking wave, he wondered if he would ever make the sanctuary of the lagoon. Somehow he did. But, as Wellington observed in the aftermath of the Battle of Waterloo, it had been a close-run thing.

Transferring ducks and gear to the boat was, to put it mildly, a wet affair. This was the least of Tim's worries though. There was still the prospect of the long journey back to the boathouse. The only redeeming feature was the fact that the tide had turned. It was, nevertheless, a nerve jangling experience. Hugging the shoreline, and with rain now literally spilling from the heavens, an eternity seemed to pass before the boathouse finally came into view. Never was a simple building a more welcome sight. To say that boat and punt limped into the boathouse would be no exaggeration. As to the human occupant of the boat, he had learned a lesson that day about the vagaries of the elements. It was a lesson that he would never forget.

11

Uncle Greg and the rabbit that never was

FARMING IN IRELAND in the 1950s was a tough proposition. And I mean seriously tough. Mixed farming was still the norm and there was no single enterprise that one could point to as a real money spinner. Mechanisation on the land still had a long way to go and hard physical labour was part and parcel of most activities. For many the day started with the milking, all still done by hand on most farms with at least half a dozen cows per man before breakfast. If one was living away from home and happened to drop in for the weekend, one would be expected to fall in and do one's bit. For those out of practice with the gentle art of milking there would be one sure result. Breakfast would be taken with aching wrists and sore fingers. Then, according to season, a long day's work lay ahead.

Take sugar beet for example. It was thinned with a hoe, pulled by hand, topped by hand and thrown into a trailer by hand. A special fork was used for the job. It had bud-like ends to the prongs so that the beet would not be pierced and get stuck on them. Worse was still to come. Some autumn evening there would be a mighty stack of roots on the roadside verge and, like as not, the lorry would arrive to take it to the factory just as dusk was falling. Somewhere between ten and fifteen tons had to be forked aboard. And there was still the milking to be done. Take my word for it, tough times that only hard men could endure.

It was against this background that I really got to know my uncle Greg. He had farmed his land since still in his early twenties when he had taken over from his father. Not a big man, Greg was wiry and as strong as the proverbial ox. However arduous the task, he always seemed to approach it with a quite extraordinary degree of good humour. When time allowed he indulged in one of his two sporting passions, shooting and anything to do with horses. There was always a fair-to-middling horse in training. Not one that would ever set the great tracks of the world alight, but one handy enough to win sufficient races to pay for its keep. On the farm he was never without a more than decent half bred which, when the spirit moved him, he would ride bareback across the fields.

Greg was unquestionably the most courageous rider it has ever been my pleasure to watch. Many a time I saw him riding at full pelt, taking five foot thorn hedges with gay abandon. If, however, he had been asked to choose between his horses and his shooting he would, I suspect, have opted for the shooting, although it would have been a close-run thing.

Greg's farm, large for its day, was run along fairly typical lines. In addition to the dairy herd and the followers, there was a fine spread of tillage. In fact it took up more than half the acreage. Strips of wheat or barley, all spring set in those days, were interspersed with beet and turnips and, of course, the obligatory acre of spuds. Then there was the plot of oats to keep the equine contingent happy. Such conditions meant that pheasants were more than adequately catered for. These were all truly wild birds. During the period of which I write there was precious little in the way of game bird release taking place in Ireland. The era of the great estates and their armies of gamekeepers had passed into history and another decade or more would pass before a new shooting order in the form of the gun club movement took root.

In his youth Greg had further catered for the needs of pheasants by setting a number of small groves around the farm. These averaged no more than half an acre each but they provided roosting quarters in a countryside which, over the years, had become perilously short of trees. The sad reality was that, since the 1930s, the economic situation had been such as to demand the felling of fine elms and oaks to provide fuel for the winter months. On most farms the kitchen fire also doubled as the focal point for cooking. A large cast iron structure incorporating a swivel was used to hang enormous cooking vessels over the fire. Apple tarts and similar goodies were baked by putting them in sealed containers and then covering them with the glowing embers. At the side of every fireplace there was room for a wooden bench. Here, on cold winter nights, the family would sit and chat. Television wouldn't have stood a chance.

It was uncle Greg and another uncle, Jim, who farmed nearby, who together passed on the shooting bug to me. Both of them shot with hammer guns, probably made in the late 1800s. They had Damascus barrelling which gave them a brownish appearance. Greg's was an especially handsome gun, the first that I had ever seen with an under lever.

Given the choice of shooting grounds I would always opt for Greg's farm over Jim's. There was, and still is, a simple reason for this. Way down at the back of the farm lies a bog. Bisected by a stream the land there is so low-lying that it has defied every attempt to drain it. Whilst nowadays it does not hold as much water in the winter as it used to do, it still draws in a multitude of duck when the rains come in earnest. Only the geese no longer come. In times past the music of the White-fronts in the darkening sky would cause us to crouch that little bit lower in the reeds and hope and pray that they would come whiffling down. Those were sights and sounds that never failed to thrill.

For Greg the demands of farming were such that, other than for an occasional evening, shooting was confined to Sundays. And even then there was first the milking to be attended to until the cows were dried off, usually towards the end of October.

According to season he would pursue the duck and the snipe, the pheasant and the partridge. Lucky man that he was, he had more than sufficient of all of them on his own land to meet his needs. Poaching was rarely a problem as there were few shooters in the locality in those days. The odd smart man who wanted to acquire a pheasant or two would bide his time and wait until opportunity for a quick incursion presented itself. This, most likely, would be on the very occasional Saturday afternoon when Greg had a horse running in Clonmel or Gowran Park. On those days the farm would be deserted as the entire family took time off to attend the races.

I, incidentally, had a very special job on those occasions. Greg would present me with a substantial bundle of fivers, serious money at the time when it is recalled that a farm labourer received the princely sum of three pounds for six days of hard labour. My instructions were always the same. Circulate casually through the betting ring putting on a fiver here and a fiver there. Greg always seemed to know when his horse was going to win and it was vital that the good gentlemen of the turf were not aware of the fact. To this end one never approached neighbouring bookies as this would surely give the game away. So, having placed a bet, which for some strange reason was always around 9–2, one walked around trying to look casual before plunging again. And this tactic would be repeated until the bundle of fivers had all, hopefully, been wisely invested.

During the close season it was Greg's custom on Sunday afternoons to take a walk around the farm. Rabbits, all too plentiful at the time, were the subject of his special attention on these jaunts. They were highly regarded by country dwellers and in many a household rabbit was on the menu at least once a week. In consequence there was little difficulty in disposing of the Sunday afternoon bags. Indeed it was not unknown for a neighbour or two to call in the evening to see if Greg had any rabbits going abegging.

One thing that could be said with certainty, or at least very near certainty, was that these Sunday afternoon outings were pretty routine affairs. Not the kind of sport that raises the adrenaline levels and sets the pulse racing. Until, that is, one fateful Sunday in the sunny month of August.

Hay figures large in the drama that was to unfold that afternoon. In those days it was usually cut in July when it was good and heavy. Sometimes it might be left until August. Then began the long and tedious business of saving it, a process that would not end until it was safely stored in the barns. First of all it had to be turned for wind and sun to do their job. Weather permitting this took place every day for four or five consecutive days. Then it was forked into small heaps commonly referred to as hens. Some days later the hens were used to construct much bigger heaps known as cocks. A cock, or hay cock, could be six or seven feet in height and weigh many hundredweights. They were usually left in the field for a week or two before being drawn to the barns.

By the time that the cocks were ready for removal it was well into August and the grass in the field had grown again to ankle height. Rabbits had a particular liking for this last flush of the year. Maybe it was because the surrounding fields, which had been grazed all summer, only had coarse vegetation on offer. Anyway, the August hay fields with the cocks still in position provided wonderful rabbit shooting for a few short weeks. The cocks were invaluable as their random distribution allowed one to creep undetected into range.

On the late summer afternoon in question, Greg had accounted for five or six rabbits and the carcasses had been safely stored under hay cocks to hide them from the prying eyes of grey crows. They would be collected at a later hour. There was just one more field to try. Located at the far side of the farm it was a long, relatively narrow field some twenty acres in extent. Sloping gently down to the bog, it was a place much favoured by rabbits, perhaps because of the sandy soil which made burrowing easy. A matter, very definitely, of keeping the best wine until last.

Arriving at the field gate Greg was amazed to find that there was not so much as a single rabbit to be seen. Usually the place would be teeming with them. In fact it was not unusual to shoot four or five in as many minutes. Despite this setback he decided to proceed with his normal plan of campaign. This consisted of a slow and careful approach to the hay cock which allowed the best view around the field. From this vantage point he would, after a couple of minutes, peep around the hay hoping to see an unsuspecting victim in range. This time however victim there was none. About to leave, Greg's attention was drawn to a hay cock some forty yards away. There had been, or so he thought, the slightest flicker of movement on one side at the back of the cock. He watched and waited. Sure enough there was another brief flicker of movement. A slim, darkish object moved rapidly upwards and then disappeared. For no better reason than that he was out rabbit shooting, and rabbits were usually the only inhabitants of the field, he assumed that he had seen the movement of a rabbit's ear. He raised the gun and waited. He did not have to wait long. Momentarily the 'rabbit's ear' appeared once more. In that instant second, he fired.

Two things now happened simultaneously. They were not things however of which Greg in his wildest imagination could have conceived. A strange-shaped blackish object went flying across the field and a high pitched squeal clearly emanating from one of the human female persuasion split the air. Almost immediately the source of the squeal appeared from behind the cock hopping along on one leg and continuing to make strange and unhappy noises. She was quickly followed by a male of the same species who appeared to be making rapid adjustments to his apparel. Greg, quite clearly, had boobed. And boobed big time. The rabbit's ear, or more correctly what he had assumed to be a rabbit's ear, was in fact one of a pair of stiletto heels.

It is probably best to cast a discreet veil over what this particular couple were doing behind the hay cock. Ecstasy was undoubtedly involved as was betrayed by the occasional flick of the stiletto heel.

Those were innocent times. In one sense at least. Fortunately no serious damage had resulted from the charge of No 5 shot. Most of it had, presumably, lodged in the hay. Greg brought the embarrassed couple up to the house where his lady wife dispensed tea and sympathy. Then, in a moment of weakness, he handed the young lady a ten shilling note, around sixty cents in today's currency. He also suggested that whatever the couple were doing he would regard it as a particular favour if, in future, they would do it somewhere else.

How different things are today. What compensation I wonder would a court award for a few pellets in the heel? 5,000 euro, 10,000 euro? And then of course the legal fees.

2

The last day of the season

IN OUR PART of Tipperary rough shooting is very much the norm. And the emphasis is very much on the rough, especially on the mountain reas where gorse, brambles and dense hazel clusters have to be negotiated in pursuit of woodcock and pheasant. A rea, incidentally, is an area of rough and usually infertile ground where the lower flanks of a mountain adjoin farmland. In agricultural terms it is a place to graze mountain sheep and a few cattle. Of recent years reas have, unfortunately from the shooter's viewpoint, become a bit scarce. This is because, being essentially marginal land, they are much sought-after by foresters. Indeed many of our finest local reas are now covered with the abominable Sitka spruce. Few trees, to my knowledge, are less attractive to game.

In Ireland all shooting seasons for game birds close on 31st January so there is an imperative in finding a few hours for a final walkabout with the dog on that day. Then, custom demands, it is off to the local for a jar or two of the black stuff and a chat about the good and not-so-good days of the passing season.

Most years, it has to be admitted, the sport on that final day has rather more of a whimper than a bang about it. Several elements combine to ensure this. The surviving cock pheasants (hens are not shot in Ireland except under special permit) are now seasoned veterans in the matter of discreet departure. In fact anyone that ends up in the bag on the 31st January must stand (or rather lie) condemned of an act of extreme carelessness. Then there is the weather. Likely as not, cool, breezy and either wet or very wet. Most years an excess of surface water means that snipe, teal and mallard have just too many places to go. As for the woodcock, ever a bird of mystery, it might condescend to be in one of its favoured haunts or, there again, it might not. A par score for this final round up is usually something like a couple of teal and a snipe or a mallard and a woodcock.

In 2009 the 31st January fell on a Sunday. Unusually it dawned bright and cold with the car thermometer registering a temperature of -3°C. On that day my first allotted task was to acquire a couple of snipe. Or at least try to acquire same. The previous afternoon, long-time shooting companion, Mick, and I had scoured some wild glens on the Tipperary/Waterford borders in a not very successful search for woodcock. A lot of hard walking had resulted in no more than three or four flushes. In the course of our travels Mick had asked me to get him the snipe if at all possible. The previous October his lovely Black Labrador had died suddenly and it was only now that he had found a worthy replacement. Mick is big into dogs and he reckons that there is nothing better than a snipe for the initial stages of training a retrieving dog. The same snipe, I would add, is likely to be returned to the deep freeze on a number of occasions before it finally disintegrates.

Early on that Sunday morning there was no point in trying the local bogs for snipe. At -3°C no self-respecting member of the species would be in residence. The best bet, I decided, was a shallow stream not too far from the house. Often as not a few snipe are minded to locate on the muddy edges during periods of frost. And there was no reason to suspect that they would not be present on this particular morning. Whether they were or not however was to quickly become academic. Whilst I was still the best part of a hundred yards from the stream, a pack of some twenty teal, wary as ever despite the numbing conditions, rose and then obligingly settled a few hundred yards downstream where the banks are conveniently shrouded with bushes. A change of plan was clearly necessary. Gift horses should never be looked in the mouth, least of all on the last day of the season. Anyway there were other places that could be searched for snipe later in the day.

A wide loop across the field terminating at the bushes was the appropriate strategy. And it was successful. Mind you, the second bird, a cock, was a long shot as the current had carried the pack some distance downstream from the bushes. As it happened the shots did not disturb any snipe and there were none along the stream as I made for home.

At this juncture that curse of the shooting classes, domesticity, intervened and it was not until the early afternoon that I was able to continue my quest for snipe. By then the temperature had risen quite significantly so there was a better than evens chance that a few would have returned to the rushy bogs. Leahy's bog was the obvious first port of call. Somewhere around eight acres in extent and located in a hollow, it has proved undrainable. Even in mid-summer the ground is more than a shade spongy underfoot. Summer grazing keeps the rushes in some sort of check so that the ground cover is just about the right height to keep snipe happy. They tend to avoid high vegetation which stacks the odds in favour of foxes and other ground predators.

There were only five snipe in the bog and two of them were well out of range. Of the remainder, two fell and, if the truth be known, I should have bagged the third as well. Mission accomplished, I had just made my way to the edge of the bog when a low pitched 'cok, cok' betrayed the presence of a nearby pheasant. The sound emanated from a cluster of blackthorns about half way down the northern edge of the bog. Ordinarily I would have kept going as the chance of finding a pheasant without a dog is negligible. But it was the last day of the season and, as the saying goes, hope springs eternal.

It was in the course of the next five minutes that two events occurred which made me think it worthwhile to record this story. Retracing my steps through the rushes I was alerted by a slight rustle a few yards to my right. In a rather too leisurely manner, a woodcock rose and made an unsuccessful attempt to depart the scene. Poor fellow, if it had not been for that Judas of a pheasant he would certainly have spent the rest of the day in rather more congenial surroundings than the cold depth of a game bag. For some inexplicable reason woodcock that flush in the open tend to take a more relaxed view of life than those disturbed in woodland and scrub. This particular unfortunate fell near to the blackthorns in which the pheasant was concealed. I was in the act of picking it up when the said pheasant, possibly suffering a panic attack due to the proximity of my shot, burst from the bushes and took a suicidal line straight towards me. Fortunately I had the presence of mind to pull the second trigger. Not often, it has to be said, does one bag a woodcock and a pheasant in quick succession without the aid of a dog.

The day was definitely improving. It was to get still better. A few friends had been invited to join my sons and me for a final crack at the duck. We have three flight ponds but at this end of the season we only shoot the two at the opposite extremities of the farm. The large central one is left as a sanctuary after Christmas. It had not been a great year for duck shooting. Incessant rain throughout November meant that they had simply too many places to visit. Then, to compound matters, in December one of the coldest spells in living memory caused the ponds to freeze up. Despite breaking the ice every morning and administering a generous dollop of barley, we only succeeded in attracting a handful of mallard and the odd teal. Ten days previously six guns were only able to account for four mallard.

A little before dusk the two sons and Jim, being considered the fittest of the assembly, were dispatched to the lower pond – a half mile hike across some seriously rough ground. Going is bad enough, coming back in pitch darkness is, to put it mildly, an interesting experience, especially when carrying a gun and a couple of pairs of duck. John, Mick and I took up positions in the furze that grows in profusion along one bank of the top pond. As usual I warned the lads about the long eared owls. In the early dusk they have a habit of beginning their nocturnal hunting trips by flying a couple of circuits of the pond. I think that they have 'copped on' to the fact that there are rats about because of our generosity with the barley.

We did not have long to wait. The snipe had barely stopped screeching in the darkening sky when a lone mallard drake came hurtling in without bothering to engage in a precautionary circuit. He was followed in fairly rapid succession by four small flights of 5, 4, 3 and 2, though not in that particular order. They too, in carefree manner, came straight in. I could have no complaint about the quality of the shooting that evening. Not a single bird escaped. Meanwhile down on the lower pond only the odd shot punctuated the evening stillness.

Half an hour later the two groups met up, we with our fifteen mallard, they with a mallard, a teal and a whinge or two about where most of the barley must have been scattered. A great end to the season, at least for our group! It will be though, I suspect, many a long year before the passing season delivers with similar generosity.

3

The bilingual dog

FIRST AND FOREMOST Hector was a Scotsman, something of which he was inordinately proud. Tall, a little over six feet in height, and wiry, he was a typical son of the Highlands. Though well into his forties there was little to betray the fact that he was nearing the end of his fifth decade other than a few strands of silver in his bushy red brown hair. Strong and superbly fit he was still more than a match for much younger men when it came to walking the hills and glens of his native land.

If one wanted to find a term that best described Hector, 'self-sufficient' would probably come nearest to the mark. A man of few words, he was never happier than when out in the wild country with his beloved dogs at heel. He had never married, much to the disappointment of more than one local lass, and despite being well into his middle years he was still regarded as something of a 'catch' in the locality. But the dogs, a surprising mixture of collies, setters and springers, were his greatest love. By profession he was a sheep farmer and a more than dedicated one. His sheep grazed over a vast acreage of mountain and moorland and the collies never failed to marshal them according to his command. All commands were issued in Hector's native tongue. Indeed he had never owned a dog, or so he said, that understood a single word of English. To them the conversation of the Anglo Saxons who came into contact with their master was no more than sounds in the same way that the whispering of the breeze in the heather or the lapping of waves on the loch were sounds. From early puppyhood they had to learn and respond to such words as *falbh* (go), *stad* (stop), *a mach* (out) and so on. Strangely, none of them was ever given a name. All were simply addressed as *madadh* (dog). But there never seemed to be a problem. By the slightest change in the inflection of Hector's voice each *madadh* knew that he, and he alone, was being addressed.

The early autumn was the busiest time of year for the collies. Day after day they assisted Hector with the annual round-up. Even for the hardiest of mountain sheep, the hills are a tough place to live once winter begins to descend. Most years it took a few weeks to assemble them in the secure pastures of the valley. From dawn to dusk every glen and every hillside was searched diligently. Hector, like all his race, was a canny man and could not rest easy until every income unit had been safely retrieved. In fairness though, like all good farmers he had more than a passing concern for the welfare of his animals and would not entertain the possibility that any of them might die a lingering death when winter blizzards swept across the hills.

During those long autumnal days on the hills Hector was also busy making mental notes for his winter 'vocation'. Whilst the collies would soon be granted their annual furlough it would not be long before the springers would be called upon to earn their keep. The wild land upon which the sheep grazed was studded with countless small lochs and ponds.

As the days of autumn passed the smallish local populations of mallard and teal on these waters were, on an almost daily basis, augmented by migrants. Goldeneye, tufties and an assortment of other duck winged in from their northern breeding grounds. Then there were the wild geese: Pinks in ever-increasing numbers, and Greylags, all intent upon finding rather more congenial surroundings than those that they had not long vacated. Unlike the duck the geese would not stay long. The fertile grain fields along the east coast commanded their presence and they would shortly obey that command.

Shooting men, and lest we be accused of sexism, shooting women, fall basically into two categories. These are based upon the individual's view of the canine world. There are those for whom the dog is an essential companion in the field but for whom the work of the said companion is secondary to the adrenaline-stimulating challenge of the chase. And, there are those for whom the workings of the canine companion, whether in the matter of finding or retrieving, are paramount. Hector, without question, belonged to the second group. As many could testify, he was no slouch with the gun but it was the performance of his dogs that really mattered to him. His setters, on command, quartered the heather with what could only be described as military precision. On making a find they would freeze in the elegant posture of their kind, one often backing up the other. Some setters may be described as 'sticky'... reluctant to move and make that final act of flushing the find. Not so Hector's. As far as he was concerned, a setter's role did not cease upon making a find. Equally important, it had, on instruction, to complete its job spec and get the quarry airborne.

But whatever about his obvious affection for his setters there can be little doubt but that the springers were his favourites. He enjoyed their bouncy companionship, their ceaseless energy and the zeal with which they went about their work. And, above all, he admired their courage when it came to retrieving duck from the coldest and wildest mid-winter lochs.

When time allowed Hector supplemented his income by acting as ghillie for the shooting parties that stayed at the local hotel. Grouse, while not exactly plentiful in the area, were sufficient in numbers to provide a few days' walked-up sport. Few, from Hector's point of view, was the operative word as he found it hard to drag himself away from the essential task of rounding up his flock.

Later in the year he had more time on his hands and the springers were rarely short of work. At morning and evening flight they dutifully retrieved the fallen. Between times they were likely to be engaged in their favourite task of terrorizing the woodcock that lurked in the plentiful scrub scattered across the mountain fringes. And, whatever the job spec of the day, they performed superbly, responding always to their master's quiet and relaxed words of command. Hector's clients never ceased to be amazed at the workings of his dogs. Indeed they were frequent topics of conversation when the shooters gathered around the hotel fire for a spot of Highland hospitality at the conclusion of a day's sport. Until, that is, one fateful day.

It was a morning in late December and a roaring north-easterly had driven fowl of every description to the comparative calmness of a broad, shallow loch which Hector and his clients were flighting. As well as the normal consignment of dabblers, the ferocity of the wind had brought inland duck whose preference would be to spend their lives well out to sea. The bag had mounted steadily and the springers had had one of those non-stop mornings retrieving. Towards the end of the flight one of the pair appeared to have damaged a front paw clambering over the rocks. Hector had immediately taken it back to the dog box and given it a good rub down before returning to the fray. The remaining *madadh* had, meanwhile, carried on with his work. He was, however, growing visibly tired. A combination of wind, waves and the bitter coldness of the day was taking its toll.

When Hector got back to the loch there was still a wigeon to be retrieved. Already some eighty yards from the shore, it was being carried further out by the wind. The guns, by this time finished, were assembled and as the dog had not, despite their urgings, gone out on the retrieve, the group were awaiting the return of Hector. Sizing up the situation Hector immediately issued the necessary word of command. But *madadh* did not move. For the first time in his life Hector was faced with an insubordinate canine. Gently he repeated the word of command. Again *madadh* did not move. Once more, again gently, the command. Once more there was no response. Hector, quite clearly, had entered new and unfamiliar territory. And, to make matters worse, there was an audience. Moreover it was an audience, human nature being human nature, which was thoroughly enjoying the show.

There is little doubt but that it was the presence of an audience that brought the matter to an unexpected conclusion. From Hector's viewpoint the ownership of a disobedient *madadh* was unthinkable. To be seen to be the owner of a disobedient *madadh* was something he simply could not handle. For the first time in his life, Hector thoroughly lost the plot. His face reddened, the veins in his neck bulged and his fists tightened in anger. To his eternal regret, words passed his lips that he had never used before. 'Get the f★★★★★ duck you wee b★★★★★★,' he roared at the sinner. Immediately and to his credit *madadh* did just that. A first for him too, it must be observed because without the benefit of a translation service, he had responded accurately to an alien tongue. Within minutes he was presenting the wigeon to his master.

Composure quickly restored, Hector took the bird and handed it to one of the guns. 'Same time tomorrow morning,' he called back as he strode over to his van. *Madadh* followed, just a little further than the usual respectful pace behind.

Rumour has it that Hector and *madadh* had a long *tête à tête* that evening on the subject of industrial relations. Agreement, it seems, must have been reached. Hector never again addressed *madadh* in the tongue of the foreigner and, by way of reciprocation, *madadh* never again attempted to renege on his contractual obligations.

4

An addition to the script

AT THE BACK of our farm, the land falls away to a mini wilderness which we call the bog. Some of it belongs to us and the remainder to two neighbours. Strictly speaking it is not a bog at all, more a low lying wettish place that holds a few snipe during the autumn and winter months. It has one special feature: it is home to a number of species of wild orchid. There are plenty of patches of rushes and clumps of furze around the edges. In the neighbours' sections there are also some stands of hazel.

Over the years, and according to the state of the exchequer, we dug out and developed a number of flight ponds in our part of the bog. All are quite shallow, averaging around three feet in depth, and each has a large central island. This latter feature is essential if released mallard are to have any hope of surviving until it is time to face the guns in September. Despite our best efforts at control, foxes are much too plentiful so we have to do all in our power to keep the young ducks away from the banks of the ponds.

We buy in 300 six-week-olds as early as possible in July and from day one they are trained to make the islands their home. Morning and evening I wade across and scatter a liberal quantity of barley all over the islands. My philosophy is simple. The more time that they spend feeding and loafing on the islands, the less time they will have to embark upon suicidal forays into the bog. By and large this works quite well and the majority do tend to spend most of their time on the islands. There are always, needless to say, a few stupid ones who fail to be satisfied by the arrangements. They don't tend to last too long.

The islands have a secondary value in that they provide nesting sites. There is a good tangle of grasses and other vegetation present on two of them and most years six or seven broods emerge. Our one disappointment is that some of the mothers insist upon taking their ducklings to a nearby river once they are a few days old.

Most years the new recruits are flying strongly by mid-August and there is constant traffic between the ponds and surrounding barley stubbles. It is then our practice to give them a further few weeks grace before we have the first shoot.

Two years ago we opted for the last Saturday of September to start proceedings. It was a particularly balmy evening and the usual troops had been ordered to assemble in the farmyard at 5pm. This would allow adequate time to walk down to the bog and take up positions by 5.30pm. Since dusk does not descend hereabouts until around 8pm at this time of year, this early start requires some explanation. As with many human endeavours, things can and do go wrong and we have to learn from our mistakes. The timing of the first shoot was a case in point. In the early days we would ensure that all the guns were in place just as dusk was beginning to fall. A springer was then used to flush the ducks. From a purely shooting point of view this worked almost too well. Unaccustomed to the sudden rude disturbance the duck would stay in the air and provide plenty of sport. Then after a while the majority of the survivors would begin returning to the ponds and we would stop shooting.

Unfortunately though, a sizable minority, obviously disorientated by their first exposure to a barrage of fire, would land literally anywhere. And where they landed they were likely to spend the night if, that is, they were fortunate enough to escape the attentions of Reynard. It became clear that we were losing birds quite unnecessarily. As a result, the timing of the first shoot was brought back.

Essentially, it was decided, the shooting and pick up should be completed whilst it was still bright. Then all but one would leave the place. The task of the man who remained was to do a quick tour of the bog and surrounding fields accompanied by a dog. Any birds that had landed would thus be flushed and hopefully make it back to the ponds. This procedure works quite well and most years upwards of a dozen mallard are driven back into the fold.

On the evening in question, the party, which consisted of sons Rupert and Paul, together with our good friends John and Philip and myself, were in high spirits. It is always good to get back to the serious business of shooting in the wild places after a long lay-off. The dogs, too, were entering into the spirit of the occasion, prancing around as we made our way down to the ponds in the evening sunshine.

As soon as everyone had taken up their allotted positions in the reed beds, Rupert sent his springer, Willow, into the biggest of the ponds. By this time of year most of the duck have gravitated towards this pond, probably because it gets the heaviest feeding. With a positive roar of wings and a chorus of alarmed quacking, the mallard were in the air and the shooting was fast and furious. In addition to the released birds there are always twenty or thirty wild ones as well. Once feeding starts in July they quickly move in and become quite tame. There is always a handful of teal as well. These are local bred birds. We rarely see migrant teal much before the second half of October.

The aim at the first shoot is to bag somewhere between 25 and 30 so each gun knows that he must stop shooting when he has five or six down. Within twenty minutes the shoot was over and most of the duck had been retrieved. As the search for the remainder continued, the survivors were already beginning to pitch back into the ponds. I had accounted for all of mine and was about to pull out when, a hundred yards or so to my right, Philip let out an ear-splitting roar. He had been searching a particularly heavy clump of rushes for a wounded bird. As I turned in response to this unexpected event, I saw that he had started to run in my direction, tearing off his clothes as he went and continuing to make a lot of very unhappy noises. Meanwhile, oblivious to this strange turn of events his Labrador, Bill, was continuing to search for the missing duck.

It had become something of a tradition at this first shoot of the year to take a group photo complete with dogs and the slain. I thus had the camera to hand. Sensing that posterity would be disappointed if I did not provide a permanent record of this unusual addition to the script, I grabbed the camera and succeeded in taking two photos. Philip was very near to me for the second of these. Whilst it is probably best to leave precise details of the recorded image to the reader's imagination, I have it on good authority that in the terminology of the photographic profession it almost qualified as a full frontal.

At this juncture I have to confess to uncontrollable mirth, something shared by the rest of the crew. It is not everyday that one gets to see a sixteen stone man in his prime tearing half naked across a bog uttering a range of indecipherable sounds.

Two things then happened simultaneously. I stopped laughing and discovered the reason for Philip's unusual behaviour. As he sped past me I felt a sharp sting on my forehead just between my eyebrows. Philip was positively covered with wasps and one of them had decided to jump ship and pay me a visit. They were in his hair, under his few remaining garments, in fact literally everywhere. When he finally got rid of them he was not a happy man. It appeared that as he searched for the mallard he had put his foot into what he thought was a large ball of dead mosses. In fact it was a wasps' nest and its inhabitants were rather less than pleased with him.

After the shock Philip recovered somewhat and was just about able to see the funny side of things. But that was not quite the end of the matter. He had received over twenty stings and at home later that evening felt decidedly unwell. In fact a number of days were to pass before he was once more his normal bouncy self.

A few days later the photos came back. One of the group suggested to Philip that, suitably adorned, with holly in all the right places, they might make unusual and interesting Christmas cards. I will not repeat his response to that particular suggestion. In fact there was only one thing a good Christian could do. The photos were duly destroyed. But from time to time we remind Philip of his gala performance on that particular evening.

5

One boundary day

'BETTER THAN any Christmas present,' said Myles, 'We never before touched seventy, let alone going over the eighty mark. Can't see it happening again for a long time though.' His colleagues, all smiles, nodded in agreement. But over by the incubation shed Santa Claus, in the person of gamekeeper, Eric, appeared rather less than happy. In truth he was doing his best to hide a scowl as he said goodbye to the shooting party.

I must however go back a number of years. As estates go, Sir Nick's would probably be best described as bijou. Located in the heart of the West Country it extended over little more than a couple of square miles. The pheasant shoot was its owner's pride and joy. To be quite honest though there was more than a touch of the curate's egg about it. In its favour was the fact that there was no shortage of mature oak woodlands, nearly four hundred acres in all, nicely distributed through rich agricultural land in blocks of varying size. Another plus was the farming regime. Effectively all the ground was given over to cereal production. On the down-side, much of the land was rather flat, making it nearly impossible to provide genuinely high birds on most of the drives. In this respect there was one redeeming feature. The biggest parcel of woodland was divided in two by a deep cut valley. As long as the wind behaved itself it was possible to drive this area in both directions on what Sir Nick liked to refer to as the big days.

The estate had in fact been considerably larger when his father inherited it. However, a love of the good things of life, coupled with rather too many injudicious investments at such centres of equine excellence as Catterick and Kempton Park had precipitated a number of enforced sales. As a result Sir Nick's birthright was such as to keep him just below the lifestyle which he believed to be his rightful due.

In passing, mention must be made of the good gentleman's title. His father had always insisted upon being addressed as Sir Tom. Whether he was actually entitled to this particular accolade was not altogether clear. There were certainly some locals, whom he regarded as being of a scurrilous and rebellious nature, who held that it was no more than self-delusion. Few, though, had the courage to address him simply as Tom. To do so was to invite the steely stare and the pregnant silence until he was afforded the correct recognition of his status.

When the aforementioned good things of life propelled Sir Tom to an early grave, Nick as his only son took over the reins. Probably for no better reason than force of habit, he was, from the start, afforded the same mode of address as his father. And, whilst he was never known to make an issue of the matter, Nick came to expect this same recognition of what he liked to think of as his true standing in life.

Being passionate about his shooting, Sir Nick rarely missed one of the big days. Big, incidentally, translated in theory into three hundred birds for a team of eight guns. There were though those days on which, due mainly to the incompetence of the shooting party, it was a struggle to get up to much over two hundred. Altogether there were sixteen big days and the revenue from these, together with the rental for the arable land, was just about sufficient to keep the wolf from the door.

The shoot was run by the ever-reliable Billings brothers, Eric and Ron. The duo, both confirmed bachelors, literally came with the estate having served Sir Tom for many years. Ron was undoubtedly the driving force behind the operation. As well as organising the shoots he was much involved in rearing the pheasants. Eric was a first class gamekeeper skilled in all aspects of his work. It was a rare day on which the guns could justifiably complain of a lack of birds.

It was Ron who first suggested that, in addition to the big days, the estate's cash flow could be enhanced by incorporating a number of boundary days into the annual programme. Always short of a few shillings, Sir Nick was only too happy to go along with the proposal. Essentially a boundary day would consist of fifty pheasants for ten guns. Divided into two groups they would alternately drive and stand. Initially the charge per gun was seventy five pounds. But, in a comparatively short period of time, the shoot became extremely popular and those economic laws that govern the market place came into effect. Within two years there was more than a sufficiency of punters happy to part with one hundred pounds and, not long afterwards, one hundred and fifty for the privilege of shooting on the estate. Local dog enthusiasts were only too delighted to get the chance of helping with the beating and picking up. As a result the running costs of the shoots were not that high.

A typical boundary day translated into five drives, if some of them could be so called, three in the morning and two in the afternoon. For Eric the vital challenge was to keep the shooting parties on the go for the full day. And, as much as possible, to keep them away from the best drives reserved for the big days. Fortunately for him there were so many blocks of woodland that this regime usually created few problems. Whilst the precise format varied little from shoot to shoot, there was a certain amount of making it up as it went along. It was really a matter of taking the guns over fairly fertile ground where they might be expected to bag ten to fifteen birds and then follow this up with an expedition to an outlying wood (which was never fed) which likely held no more than an ancient rooster or two. So skilful had he become at this type of manoeuvring that, come the last drive, there would be somewhere around forty pheasants in the bag. He could then decide upon the patch that would likely, in the final hurrah, bring the total to the magic figure of fifty. That last drive was always, to some extent, in the lap of the Gods. But Eric was never too bothered if the final total exceeded the target by a few birds. Indeed it suited him for this to be the case as, not infrequently, a grateful team of guns was likely to cross his palm with paper. And anyway, a cynic might observe, they were Sir Nick's birds not his.

As the years passed the boundary shoots continued to enjoy a high level of support, mainly but not exclusively from sportsmen living within a thirty or so mile radius. Then, literally out of the blue, an event took place which was to have a profound effect on the estate and, most especially, on the shoot. By now well into his fifties, Sir Nick got married. Nothing too unusual about that it might be observed, after all people get married every day. Few, though, select a wife such as he did. First of all she was a denizen of the United States. Nothing whatsoever wrong with that. But, secondly, she was as militant an anti as one could have the misfortune to meet. In her time she had, at home in Idaho, been prominent in campaigning against most things that country folk take for granted. Trapping, squirrel hunting, fish farming, you name it, at some stage it had been the focus of her not inconsiderable ire.

But as far as the good Sir Nick was concerned, besotted as he was, Millicent could do no wrong. So when she indicated her displeasure concerning the shoot, and more especially her husband's participation in it, he readily withdrew from an active role in the proceedings. Such, it may be observed, is the all conquering power of love. He did however point out that if the shoot were to be discontinued, finances would be seriously affected and their lifestyle, such as it was, blighted. Now whatever her convictions, Millicent was a realist. A compromise of sorts was thus agreed. As long as he had nothing to do with it, the shoot could continue. And, as much as possible, the love birds would be absent from the estate on big days so that she would not have to endure what she referred to as the sights and sounds of slaughter. The only question to be addressed was who would take on overall responsibility for the shoot and ensure a similar cash flow to that presently pertaining.

An answer to that particular question was not long in coming. There were few in the locality unaware of Sir Nick's predicament. One evening he received a phone call from a regular at the big days. Giles Montague was rich, in fact very rich. No one knew how he made his money. It was something to which he never alluded other than, on the odd occasion, describing himself as an entrepreneur. Giles had a proposition which Sir Nick could not turn down. Essentially he would take on the shoot, pay a more than respectable annual premium for the privilege and also a share of the profits above a certain figure. In addition, even though the old reliables, Ron and Eric, were getting on in years, he would retain their services and build a degree of profit-sharing into their contracts.

When, later, Giles put the proposition to the brothers, he had only one stipulation. He wanted an increase in the number of boundary days. The shoot, he explained to them, had to give him a good return on his investment. And, he stressed, the more money the shoot made, the more they would get. Not unwillingly, the two old retainers signed up for the new regime.

The transition to the new order proceeded smoothly and, initially, everything was much as before. The big days, now rather more expensive, continued as usual and, as agreed, the number of boundary days was increased substantially. But for the likes of Myles, who we met at the beginning of this tale, and who organised a team of friends for regular visits to the estate, a small but subtle change soon became apparent. Eric, now with a sound financial motive to conserve stocks, was becoming less and less generous once the bag had topped the forty mark. Final bags in excess of fifty became something of a rarity and many a day ended with a total kill somewhere in the mid-to-high forties. And when on such occasions grumbling became apparent, he always had his answer. 'There was more than enough birds,' he would say, 'you just need to shoot a bit straighter.'

Myles and his team continued to pay their usual two or three visits to the shoot each season. Sometimes they just exceeded the prescribed fifty birds, but more commonly they tended to end up a little short of par. Then came that never-to-be-forgotten day in mid December. It was the team's second visit of the season and prospects were not great. Heavy overnight rain had left the covers sodden and a blustery wind gave the pheasants little incentive to take to the wing. The first drive of the day yielded a paltry nine birds and by lunch time just over half the target had been met. In the afternoon session, the penultimate drive had resulted in the addition of a further eight birds to the bag. The team was clearly less than happy and Eric, for the first time in ages, was faced with a dilemma. His chosen finale for the proceedings was a long, narrow strip of woodland without any great excess of ground cover. It was the sort of place that could usually be relied upon to deliver a half dozen or so pheasants. Now, clearly, this would not suffice. An added difficulty was that the sky was beginning to darken prematurely and rain was not far away.

Decision time for Eric. He was left with no option but to shoot one of the woods usually reserved for big days. But which one? The half of the big wood to the west of the deep valley had not shot particularly well on the last big day so, he thought, today it might just meet his purposes.

A question then of the best laid plans of mice and men. For reasons best known to the local pheasants, a consensus had been reached that this wood best met their roosting requirements that evening. As soon as the walking guns began their advance, the shots became aware that this was going to be a drive with a difference. Few stretches of cover were without pheasants and for both walking and standing guns the shooting was fast and furious. Walking behind the advancing line, as was his wont, Eric was powerless to reduce the barrage. Then, all too soon, at least from the point of view of Myles and his friends, it was over. In excess of fifty birds had been picked up and the dogs were still searching for more.

Back in the yard Myles's words continued to echo in Eric's ears. 'Can't see it happening again for a long time.' 'It certainly won't if I have anything to do with it,' said the gamekeeper to himself.

6

An extraordinary event near Aberdeen

WHEN IT COMES to the subject of wild geese, Irish fowlers have every right to feel hard done by. By early autumn countless thousands of grey geese, mainly Pink-feet and Greylags, lift from Icelandic breeding grounds and set out on the annual trek south. And then what do they do? Ignoring every concept of fair play, they head for Scotland and other parts of mainland UK. Ireland, for no good reason whatsoever, they choose to ignore. Take the Pinks in particular. Between 40,000 and 50,000 are likely to spend the winter in Aberdeenshire alone. In contrast, in a 'good' year some fifty or sixty may deign to head for the island of saints and scholars. More usually, no more than a dozen or so will visit Ireland. The Greylags, in fairness, display a little more generosity of spirit. After a massive decline in the wintering population to some 500 birds in the late 1950s, there has been a slow, long-term increase and presently the mid-winter population stands near to 6,000. Not enough, it has to be said, to earn a place on the annual Open Seasons Order once again, but at least providing some hope for the future.

Against a background such as this it is not surprising to find that goose-starved Irish shooters tend to head for Scotland during the autumn and winter months. And in ever-increasing numbers.

This story concerns one such group, or more accurately, half of it, who make the annual pilgrimage to Aberdeen every October. The members of the group are drawn mainly but not exclusively from a gun club based in the far south of County Tipperary. What started many years ago with an intrepid band of six now numbers up to fifteen. In a typical year a major exercise in logistics gets underway just before midnight on a Saturday. Two minibuses packed to the roof with all the paraphernalia of the fowler's profession set out on the 220 mile journey to the ferry port of Larne, north of Belfast. Then, in the early hours of Sunday morning, after a sea crossing of little more than two hours, the group disembarks at Cairnryan on the Scottish coast. The final leg of the journey to the north of Aberdeen, the best part of three hundred miles, will follow the time-honoured route through via Glasgow, Dundee and Perth.

It is usually not too far short of dusk when the travel-weary troops fall out of the minibuses at the hotel. After dinner, common sense dictates a briefish visit to the bar and no more. But common-sense is a poor bedfellow of fowlers on holiday. At 4am next day alarm clocks will make their demands and within the hour the minibuses will be on the road again. This time headed for barley stubbles or grassy fields where, hopefully, the Pinks now awakening on the sea lochs will also be minded to visit.

On arrival it is likely that dawn will still be an hour or more away. Good. There is much work to be done before the baying grey skeins start to come. Hides must be erected, nets must be camouflaged meticulously with grasses and other local vegetation and upwards of one hundred decoys set out in an alluring pattern or, more precisely, perhaps, what we humans think that geese perceive as alluring! Sometimes in the middle of all this work an early, greedy skein suddenly comes whiffling down from the still dark sky. Pandemonium inevitably ensues. Everything is dropped in a mad rush to lay hands on guns and ammunition, almost always to no avail. Summing up the situation with quite commendable speed, the geese are climbing and out of range before a shot can be fired.

In 2009 the trip to Aberdeen started as per usual. As per usual, the group was divided into an A team and a B team. The former consisted of the original six and the man who signed up in the following year. Most of the latter were, in terms of the trip, of more recent vintage. Spirits were high with the prospect of the sport to come and there was the usual banter concerning which team would end the week with the bigger bag.

Monday morning was mild and dry as the two minibuses pulled out of the hotel car park and headed in opposite directions. The two fields that our guide had located were the best part of seven miles apart. From here on the members of the B team become the centre of our focus, with their colleagues in the A team having little more than bit parts in the drama that was to unfold.

By 7am the B team had completed their preparations. As dawn came it was quite obvious that the hide blended perfectly with the long white grasses that ran the length of the boundary fence. All the decoys were in position. The sheer amount of tubular greenish droppings and grey-brown feathers adorning the stubbles augured well for coming events. Time now for a well-earned cup of coffee and a bite to eat in lieu of breakfast.

The better part of an hour passed before the first skein was to appear as so many silhouettes on the distant horizon. More soon followed. As is so often the case, if the geese decide that they really like a field, they will come in in earnest. In a short space of time, 28 Pinks had been accounted for. There was then a slight lull in the proceedings. And it was at this juncture that the team became aware that a blue vehicle was parked near the field gate. After a while the vehicle was moved to a position on the side of a nearby hill. At this stage the driver's actions were of no particular concern to the shooters.

Some minutes passed and then, to the consternation of those in the hide, a shot echoed from the hill and a bullet thudded into the ground immediately behind them. It was followed almost immediately by a second one. This time the bullet struck the ground just in front of the hide.

There was only one thing that the B team could do. Common sense dictated that they lay flat on their faces on the floor of the hide. Rifle shots continued to ring out. One shattered a stake which formed part of the fence against which the hide had been constructed. Another ricocheted off a stone in the stubbles. Convinced that it was only a matter of time before someone was hit, one member of the team covered himself with dead geese in the hope that they would take the impact of any bullet coming his way.

Help was never more urgently needed. Fortunately one of the group succeeded in contacting the A team on his mobile and quickly outlined the story of what was happening. At first the recipient of the call, perhaps not surprisingly, thought that this must be some sort of a joke. After all, people do not normally fire high-powered rifles in the direction of other people in a hide. It was not until the mobile phone was held up and he heard the sound of ricocheting bullets that he realised the seriousness of the situation. Immediately he got on to the guide who in turn contacted the police. Meanwhile the ordeal in the hide continued. So close to the occupants did some of the bullets fly that it was only by the grace of God that there was not a serious injury or worse. Hard to be certain under the circumstances but it seems that somewhere between ten and thirteen shots were fired.

Shortly afterwards the shooting then stopped as abruptly as it had started and the gunman disappeared from view. It was thought likely that he had run out of ammunition. He then made a reappearance. This time he was carrying a shotgun which he proceeded to discharge into the air. Following this he started to fire the rifle again, this time in a different direction. Quite clearly, he had a lot more ammunition than the B team thought.

At this stage, the police arrived and were able to take the now-thoroughly traumatised group to safety. When the shooting finally stopped, the police moved in and made an arrest without resistance.

Not, quite clearly, the start to a shooting holiday that the group had in mind! Seriously shaken, they were taken to the local police station in Newborough. By now it was 10.30am and the morning was already seeming like a very long one. They were destined to remain in the police station until 9 o'clock that evening, providing statements and giving evidence. But there was one question that they simply could not answer. Why did a man who had been granted a firearm certificate, and therefore could be assumed to be of sound mind, embark upon this most extraordinary course of action? The shooters were not on his land – not that that would have been a mitigating factor. They had done him no harm. In fact they had never come across him before.

In the police station it was intimated to the group that it was likely that the culprit would face a charge of attempted murder. This, it was stated, was because at the range at which the shots were fired, not even the best of marksmen could guarantee that he would not hit one of the occupants of the hide. Especially so when there were eight people quite tightly packed together.

The shooting holiday continued. It was however something of a subdued affair in comparison to former years. Between the residual trauma and further meetings requested by the police, it would be fair to say that the holiday did not qualify as a resounding success.

Almost eighteen months were to pass before the gunman was finally called on to account for his crime. Only then did the team discover that he had been an RAF pilot. In the end the charge laid against him was not one of attempted murder. This, apparently, because it may not have been possible to prove conclusively. And, in the absence of same, he could likely walk free. Instead therefore, he was charged with reckless and culpable discharge of a firearm. Five members of the B team were requested to attend the trial in Aberdeen as witnesses. The trial lasted eight days. Three of the five eventually gave evidence and spent long hours in the witness box. All were quite clear about the frightening events that took place on that October morning.

The defence, to put it mildly, was almost as extraordinary as the event itself. It centred around rabbit shooting and scaring geese from a potato plot. Since the defendant possessed a shotgun the claim that a 0.243 rifle was used for crop protection beggared belief. As to the rabbits, the mind boggles as to what would be left of one if a bullet from a rifle of this calibre found its mark. It was also claimed that the defendent had discovered that he had more ammunition for the rifle than his licence allowed and that, in consequence, he decided to use it up.

The jury did not take long to record a guilty verdict. Sentencing was put back to a later date and three weeks were to pass before the gunman learned of his fate. To those who had endured the shock of coming under fire it seemed that he received little more than a slap on the wrists. Two years' probation and three hundred hours of community service was deemed to be an adequate punishment for his crime. Justice, if such it can be called, is sometimes a very strange animal indeed.

Oh! I nearly forgot. The name of the man who could have killed my friends is Michael Sutherland. As far as I know he still lives near Aberdeen.

17

Come the dusk

YOU'VE MET Phil before in these chronicles. It was he who, one warm and sunny autumn evening many years ago, incurred the wrath of a nest of wasps. The first duck shoot of the season had just ended and the pick up was in full swing. Phil, accompanied by his Labrador, Bailey, had the misfortune to put his foot in the said nest. Suffice to say what happened next was something that that good gentleman was never likely to forget.

By profession Phil is a farmer. His lands are located in one of the most scenic parts of Ireland known as the Golden Vale. To the south of his holding, the mountains provide a dramatic backdrop, especially in summer when the high ground above the forests becomes a sea of purple heather.

For shooting men like Phil there can be few more attractive places in these islands in which to ply one's trade. Up in the mountains the red grouse, though not as plentiful as in former times, provide a few enjoyable walked up days in September. Come November the conifer plantations on the lower flanks of the hills attract ever-increasing numbers of woodcock as the days begin to shorten. By day they sleep securely in the bracken and heather which fringe the fire breaks and clearings, by night they gorge themselves on earthworms in the damper fields in the valley below. Some nest in the forests but the great majority come from far-flung breeding grounds in Scandinavia and the Baltic States. These migrants are intrepid birds. In order to get to Ireland they must negotiate two wild stretches of water. First there is the North Sea, then the Irish Sea. Most years adults outnumber juveniles in the bag, unlike the UK where juveniles predominate. This, it is reckoned, is because the juveniles are far less inclined to take on a second sea crossing and so, instead, spend the winter in Scotland.

Away from the mountains Phil and his friends spend their Sundays pursuing pheasants over rich farmland. And mallard too. Local ponds and streams can pay handsome dividends to those who visit them in the early hours before the world is fully awake. Then, to add yet greater variety, there are the snipe. No shortage of these. They have their favoured haunts in rushy fields and soft patches along the river banks.

Before the coming of the forestry there were a number of flight ponds sited at strategic intervals along the mountain fringes. These had been dug out for landlords of former eras and jealously guarded by teams of gamekeepers. If even a fraction of the stories about those gallant days are true, they must have yielded prodigious bags for his lordship and his guests.

Foresters though don't like ponds. They take up good planting ground and engender in the area a dampness which is not conducive to the growth of conifers. As a result, when a new plantation is to be established on a mountain, one of the first acts is to cut a series of parallel drains which will convey all surplus water to the rivers below. By sheer good fortune however, those who had attempted to drain the pond on what is now Phil's land succeeded in making a total botch of the job. He has, as a result, a very fine flight pond just a few fields from his house.

The events which I am going to relate took place at this pond a good number of years before the wasp incident. Since he was big enough to shoulder a gun, the pond had been a special place for Phil. Originally on open ground it had, over the years, become increasingly enclosed as the surrounding trees grew up. In terms of duck shooting it had always been what we can best describe as a slow starter. Essentially it was a rare year in which it delivered much during the early part of the season. For this a nearby river was largely to blame. Of an average year it was at its lowest in late summer and early autumn so that countless weedy sandbanks were exposed during those balmy days. Mallard had all that their hearts could possibly desire on and around the sandbanks and thus had little reason to move elsewhere. Even when the shooting season started in September they would, when disturbed, simply fly a mile or so downstream and pitch down again. This carefree lifestyle would continue until the first serious rains of autumn. Then, red water bucketing out of the forest drains would turn the river into a raging torrent in a matter of hours. Now it was time to feed the pond in earnest. Shot sparingly, it rarely failed to oblige in that twilight period when the sun dropped behind the mountain.

Later in the year migratory teal would come to the pond as well. And also the occasional shoveler. Wigeon were sometimes to be heard in the sky overhead but they never actually came in. This was probably because the water surface was not broad enough and there were too many trees around. Wigeon are birds whose preference is very definitely for wide expanses of open, shallow water.

Like many a pond in a woodland setting, the surface was almost invariably covered with a green film of algae and other aquatic plants. Very handy this. Surface tracks through the vegetation betrayed the occurrence of nocturnal visitations. Once the surface was well crisscrossed with tracks it was time to lay plans for an ambush. As is the case with all grain-fed ponds, it was vital to get there good and early on the appointed evening. Mallard are greedy creatures and they are apt to take to the wing early once their gluttonous instincts have been aroused by the golden grain.

For years Phil and his friends continued to enjoy flighting the pond. But it never dawned on them that a routine event in the life of a nearby plantation would provide them with a very real bonus. That event was the first thinning. It should have taken place around fifteen years after establishment but, for reasons that were not at all clear, the forester did not get round to the job until the plantation was twenty years old.

Initially the thinning had little effect upon the shooting other than some temporary disturbance of the duck whilst the operation was in progress. Then, one grey evening towards the turn of the year, the bonus became apparent. Because dusk threatened to descend early, the team had gathered before the appointed hour. They had taken up their positions and were still chattering when a dark object passed over their heads just above tree height. Taken by surprise no one got a good look at it. One of the assembly thought that it might have been a big bat, a comment treated with derision by his colleagues. Bats, after all, have rather better things to do with their time on cold mid-winter evenings than flying around under insect-free skies.

Then it dawned on them. The object could have been nothing else but a woodcock. The speed and direct nature of its flight were the giveaways. Woodcock were quite plentiful in some of the mature forests in the area but this was the first one, at least to their knowledge, to put in an appearance in the vicinity of the pond. Thinking about it later Phil realised that it had displayed the typical behaviour of its kind. On its evening journey from the forest it had taken advantage of a newly cut thinning line to get to its nocturnal feeding grounds. The thinning line in question had brought the woodcock down almost directly over the edge of the pond.

The following evening Phil went back to the pond to see if the woodcock would make an appearance once again. And it did. The only question now, was this a one off or was he witnessing the start of a definite flight path with all that that implied for their evening shoots?

In the fervent hope of good things to come, the team at their next meeting came to a decision. There was less than a month to go until the end of the season. They would in consequence grant safe passage to any woodcock that appeared. Better in fact to wait and see if a serious flight path was going to develop. To their delight this is exactly what happened. By the end of January and well into February the number of woodcock passing down in the failing light increased steadily. Not enormous numbers, mind you, but up to half a dozen on some evenings.

The following season the woodcock continued to take the same route over the edge of the pond with only slight variations according to the direction of the wind. Evening shoots, not surprisingly, became even more eagerly awaited events. First the woodcock would come in the early dusk and then, hardly had their flight ended, the teal would be on the move. After that when it was almost too dark to see, especially against the background of a wall of trees, mallard were likely to drop in. These latter were crafty birds which knew all about the delicate art of survival. By now well versed in the ways of mankind, they rarely left the security of sanctuary waters until the dusk was well advanced.

The number of woodcock that found their way into the bag on those evenings was never that big. At the best of times, flighting them on a winter's evening calls for no small degree of skill. Essentially we are talking snap shooting. It is usually cold, the light is poor and they come hurtling down over the trees at a rate of knots. Any lapse in concentration and the bird has gone before one has had time to shoulder the gun. In the relative confines of a pond surrounded by trees, the difficulty was further magnified. The gun, quite literally, must be moving the instant the woodcock appears. Otherwise the shot is doomed to failure.

Then came THAT evening, the one on which Phil and one of his friends hit the proverbial jackpot. It had been a cold and blustery late January day and the pair had spent a number of hours traipsing forests some distance away in search of woodcock. They were not in the best of spirits. At best the springers had flushed six or seven birds, mostly out of range, and they had only succeeded in downing a couple. Their original intention was to end the day flighting the pond but, as so few woodcock had been encountered, it was debatable as to whether it was worth the bother. Were it not for the fact that the end of the season beckoned, they would probably have headed for home.

But, with precious few shooting days left, they decided to pay the pond a final visit. And were they glad they did. Starting in the very early dusk, a positive stream of woodcock came tearing over the trees. On several occasions two came together. In the course of little more than an exhilarating ten minutes the two had accounted for nine and, as they later admitted to one another, if they had shot even half decently they would have got quite a lot more. That, however, was not quite the end of the evening's sport. Hardly had the last woodcock passed down than the first of a number of small teal packs came in and they succeeded in adding eight to the bag. Seventeen birds in all, a record for the pond.

Why the woodcock came in such numbers that evening remains a mystery. It was over 30 years ago. Never again were they known to be in such an obliging frame of mind. Thereafter it was a case of three or four as a prelude to the duck flight.

There is a final twist to this story. And for Phil and his friends it was not a happy one. Two or three years after that great evening, the *Irish Wildlife Act* was in the course of being drafted. Advisors to the Minister of the day, who quite clearly knew little or nothing about woodcock or woodcock shooting, urged him to ban flighting them at dusk. It was, so these office-bound experts said, little more than routine slaughter. One wonders if these knowledgeable gentlemen had been dragged from their comfortable, centrally heated surroundings on a viciously cold winter's evening and put standing at the edge of a forest, would they have offered the same advice? Anyway the Minister listened and when the Bill was voted into law it contained the stipulation that woodcock could not be shot after sunset. And, as every shooting man knows, no self-respecting woodcock takes to the air until well after the sun has slipped beneath the horizon.

Little remains to be said. The woodcock still pass down over the pond on their way to the valley and, as Phil and his friends settle in to await the duck, they can now only watch the black silhouettes skim by and hope that the teal will not let them down.

8

Tall pheasants

'NIGEL HAMMONDSLEY here from the Callan Bridge Estate,' said the plummy voice on the other end of the phone. 'Am I addressing Mr Matthew Gleeson?' Matt paused for a moment before replying. At 9am on a Monday morning, phone calls were usually about vegetable orders for the week or, occasionally, from a supplier threatening dire retribution if an outstanding account was not settled immediately. As a general rule it would be fair to say that such contacts did not involve persons with voices corresponding to that of the good Mr Hammondsley.

Matt, I should explain, ran a small market garden. It was a one-man business which he had taken over from his father some twenty years previously. A large part of his life centred around ensuring that, week in, week out, there was a sufficiency of cabbages, carrots and the other vegetable requirements of the shops and hotels which he supplied. He had always found great satisfaction in growing vegetables and flowering plants. It was the paperwork that he thoroughly disliked. A question of needs must, though.

He had, or so he thought, solved that particular problem when he met and married Marilyn shortly after taking over the business. It was just a stroke of good fortune that his newly-acquired lovely wife had previously managed a small office and was skilled in bookkeeping matters. Sadly, the good fortune was not to last. A little more than a year after their union had been cemented at the local registry office Marilyn disappeared from his life. In a brief note that he found on the kitchen table on a Friday evening after a long day spent on delivery runs, she indicated that she had left to begin a new life with erstwhile seed salesman, Herbert Symons. She also apologised for 'borrowings' from the business account and assured Matt that restitution in full would be forthcoming once Herbert's new business venture in Portugal took off. Matt was still awaiting the said restitution.

Matt's father possessed an ancient, single-barrelled gun which he used to protect his crops from the ravages of rabbits, pigeons and the like. It was of American origin and described in the catalogue from which it had been originally purchased as semi-hammerless. This simply meant that it had a very small hammer which could be cocked with the thumb. When it eventually came into Matt's possession the scoring on the top of the hammer had worn smooth with use. The corollary of this was that, especially of a cold morning, the hammer could slip from the thumb in the act of cocking.

On more than one occasion Matt had had his thoughts quickly concentrated when, intent upon executing a rabbit for digging up young carrots, he had blown a sizeable hole in the ground just in front of his own feet. Eventually, with budgetary matters back on track after his involuntary investment in Herbert's Portuguese business, he purchased a rather more conventional weapon. This old Birmingham gun, which was in fair condition, had a lot to do with an upsurge in his interest in sporting shooting. Pigeons, which he had formerly regarded solely as pests, now became worthy quarry whenever, for a couple of hours, he could escape the multitudinous calls of the market garden. And, through his network of contacts in farming, he managed to acquire a small amount of rough shooting. Very quickly, shooting became an important part of his life.

On the last Sunday of July each year, the major landowners in the area took it in turn to host a game fair. This event had become a major fixture in the local calendar. It was a fixture that Matt never missed. And it is here that the good Nigel Hammondsley, he of the plummy voice, enters the picture. Amongst his many tasks as estate manager for the Earl of Achill, owner of the Callan Bridge Estate, was that of organising the charity raffle when his lordship's turn came to hosting the game fair. Each landowner put up a valuable prize for the draw and the not inconsiderable proceeds were distributed amongst local charities. His lordship had donated a driven day on his shoot and Nigel was ringing to tell Matt that he was the lucky winner of this particular prize. And an excellent prize it unquestionably was. The Callan Bridge shoot, which extended over the greater part of two thousand acres, was renowned for its high birds. Invitations for one of the ten days were silently prayed for by the elite of the sporting world.

A day at Callan Bridge consisted of six drives, three before and three after a sumptuous lunch. Eight guns were involved and, whilst his lordship frowned upon the concept of bag limits, something which he regarded as being more suited to lesser shoots governed by vulgar economics, his game-keeping staff knew only too well that a bag of between four and five hundred was what they were expected to engineer. To this end, when the draw was made for pegs, Nigel somehow managed to ensure that the best shots ended up, in the main, on the most productive stands.

Matt was reasonably conversant with the shoot, having had a number of stints in the beating line down the years. On those occasions he had marvelled at the sheer heights from which the top-performing guns were able, with incredible regularity, to claw down their birds. How, he had often wondered on those days, would he fare if standing at their pegs? Whilst he had never faced driven birds he had developed into a more than proficient shot and secretly fancied his chances with the exceptionally tall pheasants that he knew would come his way.

The Tuesday before Christmas was the appointed day. The first drive, Nigel told him, would start at ten o'clock but it was usual for the guns to assemble in the stable courtyard by nine. This, he explained, was necessary to allow time for the peg draw and to run through the basic rules of the shoot. There would then be plenty of time to get everyone to his appointed peg in time for the first drive. 'I'll look forward to seeing you then,' said Nigel, 'Oh and by the way, make sure to bring plenty of cartridges.'

In the weeks that followed the shoot was seldom far from Matt's mind. On two counts he was more than determined. First of all his attire would not let him down. To this end he acquired a tweed suit, especially made for him by one of the better London tailoring houses. Expense, for the first time in his life, was not a consideration. In fact, reflecting on matters financial some time later, he realised that his fine set of London threads had cost him more than he would usually spend on clothes in two years. Then there was the matter of dealing with fast high birds bearing down on him from the front. This troubled him not a little. Proficient as he had become at most shots, these were ones of which he had very little experience. His only real contact with incoming birds related to decoyed pigeons which, of course, were losing both pace and height whereas the longtails with which he would have to deal would be doing exactly the opposite. A couple of sessions at a clay shooting range would probably have been the most sensible response to his dilemma. This however was a non-starter. There was no establishment of this nature within remotely reasonable distance and, anyway, being a one-man business, he could not afford the luxury of taking time off during the working day.

Then it occurred to him. No more than a couple of miles away a farming friend of his owned a sizeable stand of larches and spruce spreading across a hill at the rear of his property. At dusk each evening rooks and jackdaws in their hundreds came to roost here. If he were to stand in the field at the foot of the hill he could have a more than adequate supply of high birds passing over. Only problem was that their speed of flight compared poorly with that of driven pheasants. But, he thought, if he could be there on an evening on which he was facing into a stiff south-westerly, the wind-assisted birds would be travelling rather faster than usual. Jackdaws, in particular, he knew could certainly motor with the wind in their tails.

A number of weeks passed before conditions were such as to meet Matt's requirements. In early October an Indian summer was fortuitously interrupted by the equivalent of a minor hurricane which persisted for two days. The first evening proved ideal. Birds positively streamed over him from every angle. Maybe their speed was not that of pheasants but it was certainly not too far behind. Gradually his confidence grew as he learned the important lesson of not shouldering his gun until the last minute. Going home he had to smile to himself. If his friends knew what he was at they would be convinced that he was half mad. But the thought worried him not a jot. He was somewhere towards achieving his objective.

The wind was as strong as ever when he returned to the field the following evening. In this session, he promised himself, there would not be a single miss. But he had not reckoned with the wit of his 'driven pheasants'. They proved to have been quick learners. After the barrage of the previous evening the vast majority sensibly gave him a wide berth. The few shots that Matt attempted though – and they were all most certainly high and wide – found their mark.

He had hoped to repeat the rook and crow exercise one last time before his appointment at Callan Bridge. It was not to be though. In the weeks that followed, anti-cyclonic weather persisted and the cold still evenings were ill suited to his plans.

At long last the big day arrived. With growing apprehension our hero joined the other guns at the appointed hour. On the stroke of nine, the headkeeper took them through the basic drill. Shooting could commence with the whistle that sent the beating line into action. At the sound of the horn all shooting was to stop immediately and guns were to be unloaded. No ground game to be shot and no foxes. And, he requested of the assembled guns, try to keep an account of fallen birds to aid the picking-up team.

Then came the draw. Making a supreme effort to stop his hand shaking, Matt drew the number two stand for the first drive. 'Probably won't be too busy there,' the head keeper remarked to Matt, 'but don't worry you're nicely set up for the other drives.' The form, he had previously explained, was that at each drive the guns moved three pegs to the right.

The first drive was nicknamed 'The Brook' because the guns were stationed along a broad, flat valley through which a small river meandered gently. The stands were on the banks of the river. Behind them and in front of them, steep, oak-covered ground rose for well over a hundred feet. No doubt about it, Matt thought to himself, there were not going to be many low birds. Adrenaline levels in his bloodstream were now rocketing. It wouldn't be so bad, he thought, if he was by himself. But the reality was that a number of by-standers would see his every move. Forty yards to his right and forty yards to his left were stationed fellow guns. Behind each stand one or two dog handlers were waiting to pick up the considerable number of birds that were expected to fall.

The whistle sounded. All along the valley shots began to ring out. Both of his neighbouring guns were soon in action. The two of them were clearly very proficient shoots. Then his turn came. From half way down the facing slope a hen pheasant rose and took a line just slightly to his right. In comparison to other pheasants that he had seen crossing, this was definitely on the low side. He hesitated. It was an easy shot but was it a bird that should be granted safe passage? Before he could decide a shot rang out from his right. 'Sorry about that old man,' shouted his neighbour, 'I thought that you hadn't seen it.' He had little time to reflect on the incident however as a cock came hurtling towards him gaining height all the time. Instinctively he threw his gun up and fired. To his great relief it fell dead thirty yards behind him. Almost immediately he repeated the exercise with another cock following virtually the same flight line. Maybe then he relaxed just that little too much, or maybe the next bird was not travelling quite as fast. Either way it kept going, not a feather displaced.

All around the shooting continued apace. Then, just when he thought his contribution to the drive was over, he spotted a bird coming in from his left. It was exceptionally high. Resisting the temptation to shoulder his gun prematurely he took a deep breath and fired as his barrels blotted out the pheasant. Undoubtedly the tallest bird he had ever fired at, it crumpled and fell to earth. Seconds later the horn sounded. As Matt stood there removing cartridges from the breech he experienced an overwhelming sense of relief. He had acquitted himself more than adequately on this, his very first drive.

On the two remaining drives before lunch he had little time to relax, such was the number of pheasants in the air. On both occasions he started with a clean miss then gradually upped his cartridge-to-kill ratio as the drive proceeded. Miss he did from time to time and, to be honest, very badly on a couple of occasions. But overall he was more than satisfied with his performance. Whilst it was impossible to keep an accurate tally of his successes due to the extraordinary level of shooting, he knew that he had accounted for the better part of thirty birds. He had only one regret. He had not succeeded, despite a number of fair chances, of pulling off a right and left.

Matt did not enjoy lunch. Whilst everyone was extremely polite and made every effort to be friendly, he found conversation difficult. He had also become quickly conscious of the fact that his set of brand new tweeds stood out in sharp contrast to the somewhat battered appearance of those of his fellow guns. He was thus greatly relieved when, after what seemed like an eternity, the head gamekeeper entered the barn. 'Time to be on our way, gentlemen,' he announced. 'We've got to get in three more drives and the afternoon will be short enough.'

Over the course of the next two hours Matt shot, for one unused to this form of sport, with commendable skill. But the double continued to elude him. A matter, almost certainly, of trying too hard.

Now not all stories can have happy endings. But in this case Matt's venture into another world most definitely had. It was the last drive of the day. For the first few minutes very few birds came his way and a cock and a hen were all he had to show for his efforts. Then everything changed quite dramatically. In front of him lay a dense belt of rhododendrons. Without warning some dozen pheasants burst from this cover and came straight towards him. As he admitted to himself later, it would have taken considerable talent to fail with a right and left. He had the luxury of choosing his second bird from several. Two magnificent cocks lay on the ground in front of him. Better was yet to come. The survivors of that fine flush of birds had barely departed the scene when an even bigger number emerged from the rhododendrons. Again the double was little more than a formality.

Back at home some hours later Matt was slowly recovering from his roller coaster experience. It was unlikely, he knew, that he would ever again experience a day such as that. He had shot with the best and, considering his total lack of experience when it came to driven shooting, he had, he felt, acquitted himself more than adequately. There was only one problem. Where on earth would he get the opportunity to don his magnificent tweeds again?

9

The fall guy

OUR COUSINS on the other side of the Atlantic have a number of words and phrases which are far more descriptive than anything we have on offer here. 'That's the way the cookie crumbles,' is a case in point. So too is the notion of a 'fall guy'. Indeed it is a fall guy who treads centre stage in the drama which I am about to relate.

My friend Jim has a quite remarkable tendency to slot into this 'fall guy' category of humanity. And what is more he tends to do so at devastatingly frequent intervals. Hard to translate fully into the vernacular of the true Anglo Saxon, the concept of the fall guy conjures up an amalgam of images. Naïve, capable of being manipulated, the one who ends up taking the rap are some of these. Basically though a fall guy is a decent sort of man. And this just about sums up Jim.

By profession Jim is a farmer. He is also a passionate shooter. Suggest some sporting enterprise to him at short notice, a run to the coast in the wee hours for morning flight for example, or a visit to some distant bog which, the bush telegraph informs, is positively hopping with snipe and he will down everything in order to go. As Siobhan, his long-suffering wife is wont to remark, 'If I couldn't milk the cows, dehorn calves, empty the slurry tanks and fodder the stock I'd be no use here.'

Take the time that Jim acquired a new neighbour. This was back in the 1960s. Owen Morgan, a denizen of Swansea, had been persuaded by his good lady wife, after years of marriage, to leave suburbia behind and relocate in her native parish on the Cork Kerry borders. In fact he was a far from unwilling participant in the venture. Despite half a lifetime spent in the neat tree-lined avenues beyond the city centre, he had always harboured thoughts of a new beginning in the countryside. And, like many a man before him, he viewed this change through the proverbial rose-tinted spectacles. Life on the smallholding that he had acquired would be an eternity of good fresh air, gentle summer breezes, hens clucking contentedly in the yard and ducks grubbing away in the paddocks. Torrential rain, much, much more rain – and sick animals – somehow didn't figure when the rose-tinted spectacles were donned.

Owen had not been in the area long when he acquired a ·22 rifle, a weapon with which he quickly became proficient. It was a straightforward matter of needs must. His few acres were mainly given over to vegetable growing and the local rabbit population had been quick to conclude that this Welshman had converted their patch into something approaching the Promised Land.

One evening in early autumn Jim was finishing off the milking when Owen appeared in the yard. He had a proposition for the morrow and, as usual, it was a proposition that Jim could not turn down. Driving home the previous evening Owen had seen a small party of fallow deer run into a forest less than a dozen miles distant. One of these, he had decided, would be a welcome supplement to the contents of his deep freeze. This, incidentally, was a good number of years before the *Wildlife Act* became law and deer had no legal protection whatsoever. In fact many regarded them as little more than vermin. Foresters didn't like them because they damaged the young trees. Farmers with lands adjoining plantations didn't like them because they grazed away valuable spring grasses.

Jim pointed out to his neighbour that a ·22 calibre rifle was more than a bit on the light side for a beast as big as a fallow deer. This was not however something that was going to deter Owen. 'I'll only take one that is really close,' he said, 'and anyway you can bring your shotgun and a few FN slugs.' These particularly lethal cartridges were freely available in those days. If memory serves me correctly they could be purchased for half a crown each. They contained a slightly pointed and flighted lump of lead which had the potential to inflict quite horrific damage. As I recall they had two major drawbacks. The first was their trajectory. It could be erratic at times and there was no guarantee the slug would find its mark however carefully the gun had been aimed. As well as this they could not be fired through a barrel with anything more than a modest degree of choke, at least by anyone with more than a minimal regard for their continued good health.

On his visit the previous evening Owen had spotted a new and unfamiliar car in Jim's yard. It was, he discovered, a Hillman Minx belonging to Jim's mother-in-law who was staying for a few days. He had succeeded in persuading Jim that, on account of its big boot, it would be an ideal vehicle in which to transport the soon-to-be-shot deer. Rather unwillingly Jim had approached the mother-in-law and it had only been with the greatest of reluctance that she had consented to its use for the expedition. 'Don't put a mark on it or we will never hear the end of it,' Siobhan had cautioned him.

Next morning the deer hunters were on the road before first light. Their intention was to walk the forest roads and tracks until a suitable beast was located. To this end they had driven the better part of a mile into the forest and it was just about light enough to see when they parked the car at the edge of a small clearing. From this point forward the day began to deteriorate rapidly.

Before they could get out of the car they were surprised to hear the noise of a powerful engine. Someone was coming up the forest road that they had just followed. And at a considerable rate of knots. 'Probably the Special Branch,' said Jim with a twinkle in his eyes. Got it in one, as the saying goes. A rather large squad car pulled up some eighty yards from them. In it a uniformed sergeant and two plain clothes officers could be seen to be eyeing them with rather more than passing suspicion.

We are talking, I must explain, about a period during which there was quite a lot of paramilitary activity in the country. Isolated forests and mountain places were popular venues for training activities and some of them were kept under scrutiny by the forces of law and order. By sheer bad luck Jim and Owen had selected an area which, unknown to them, was the subject of long-term attention. You're probably beginning to see how well the fall guy description fits.

Unsure what to do, our two heroes sat and waited. There was clearly an animated discussion going on in the squad car. Eventually the uniformed sergeant was ordered out to investigate. As he walked towards their car, very slowly it might be noted, it was apparent that he was less than a happy man, no doubt anticipating all sorts of dire consequences when he reached them. His state of mind could not have been helped by Owen's appearance. Short and heavily built, he was sitting in the back of the Hillman attired in camouflage jacket and flak cap. His trusty ·22 lay across his lap. This godfather-like appearance was further enhanced by the dark shades which, winter or summer, the Welshman insisted upon wearing.

'Good morning lads,' said the sergeant trying desperately to maintain the obligatory stiff upper lip. 'I haven't seen ye around here before.' Relief quickly registered on his face as Jim explained why they were there and he realised that, after all, nothing nasty was going to happen to him. A few pleasantries were then exchanged before a much more relaxed custodian of law and order made his way back to the squad car. Jim drew a deep breath as he turned to his companion. 'Great start to the day,' he said, 'it can only get better now.' Little did he know.

Over the next couple of hours the two hunters searched high and low for a deer. But not a deer did they meet. Tired and more than a touch grumpy, they eventually emerged from the forest to find themselves on open mountain. Jim was about to tell his companion that enough was enough and that the only sensible thing to do was to head for home when, across the still mountain air, came the unmistakable bleating of a goat. In those days many an Irish mountain was graced, if that is the correct term, by one or more herds of feral goats. In some cases they were the descendants of ones belonging to travelling people which had either escaped or had been sent into permanent exile on the high ground.

Looking around for the source of the bleating, Jim spied an enormous puck goat standing in the heather and watching them suspiciously. A magnificent, multi-coloured animal, it had an enormous pair of horns. 'He'll do just fine,' said Owen, 'you shoot him with a slug.' 'Are you serious?' his companion replied, 'you couldn't possibly eat an old thing like that.' But Owen was not for turning. Apparently in his youth he had sampled goat flesh on more than one occasion and he was clearly intent upon doing the same again.

Resigning himself to the fact that Owen was not going to take 'no' for an answer, and by this time anxious to get home, Jim succumbed to the inevitable. He had never shot a goat before and, if the truth be known, regarded his assignment as little more than an assassination. He lined up the side of the goat's head and fired. It fell to the ground, something that surprised Jim more than a little as he was conscious that he had closed his eyes as his finger tightened on the trigger. This, however, was far from the end of the episode. Almost immediately the goat got up again and began to stagger about after the manner of a drunken man. Close inspection revealed the reason for this unexpected state of affairs. Starting between its horns, a red scar could be seen running across the top of its skull. The puck, like many a hero of Western dramas, had merely been 'creased'.

At this juncture Jim was adamant. He had had more than enough when it came to the business of executing goats. 'You want him,' he said to Owen, 'so now you can finish him off with the ·22.'

Accepting that if he wanted to dine on goat in the weeks ahead he would have to complete the job himself, Owen, like his friend before him, lined up the unfortunate animal. And then, again like his friend, he began to have serious reservations about the whole enterprise. Shooting rabbits was one thing. Shooting this rather large goat that was still walking around in circles was something entirely different. Suffice to say that he too closed his eyes at the critical moment. At no more than ten feet he registered a clean miss. Jim could take no more. Uttering more than a single expletive, which like all expletives are best deleted, he snatched the rifle from Owen and administered the *coup de grâce*.

If either of these two good gentlemen had any experience of deer stalking he would straight away have bled and gralloched the beast. In the event the carcass was, for lack of a better word, stuffed, not without some difficulty, into the boot of the Hillman Minx. Then, tired from having dragged the animal over what seemed like miles of rough ground, they flopped into the car and made for home. To say that the day had not quite gone according to plan would not understate the position.

Worse, however, was still to come. So intent had the duo been in acquiring the goat that they had taken little heed of the smell emanating from it. As any devotee of hill walking knows, wild goats do not exactly please the olfactory organs. In fact the smell is usually quite appalling and this specimen was certainly no exception. Jim positively cringed. The car, his mother-in-law's pride and joy, positively reeked of goat and he could think of no simple way of remedying the situation.

With the car windows wide open Jim drove as quickly as possible to Owen's yard where, with alacrity, the cargo in the boot was unloaded. The odour of goat remained in the vehicle. Owen's wife, Marguerite, was summoned for advice. A straight-talking lady, she told Jim exactly what he did not want to hear. 'You can try all the deodorants and perfumed sprays you want,' she informed him, 'but that car is going to smell of goat for a very long time to come. Best thing you can do is go home and tell her about it.' So that is exactly what Jim did. It is probably best to draw a discreet veil over what happened thereafter. Suffice to say that Jim's description of home life in the days that followed was particularly succinct. 'It was like,' he said, 'watching television for days on end with the sound turned off.'

Just one more thing. Some days later, having first had the good sense to check that Jim's wife and mother-in-law were out, Owen dropped over with a gift for his friend. It consisted of a well-heaped plate covered with cooking foil. On removing the foil Jim found himself the proud owner of a steaming pile of slices of rather black-looking meat. And yes, it really did smell of goat. When Owen had departed, somewhat deflated at the response to his present, Jim summoned his pointer, Bruce. 'Here you are, old fellow,' he said to his favourite dog, 'a special treat for you.' Now Bruce was a true carnivore who was wont to empty his bowl whatever offerings it contained. Clearly, though, he had not experienced goat before. He gave the heap on the plate a desultory sniff and walked away. 'It's fairly obvious that you've got a bit more sense than me,' Jim called out after the departing hound.

20

Déjà vu

I'M WRITING this narrative on Tuesday, 30th August in the Year of Our Lord 2011. Until Sunday last I was feeling just that wee bit more smug than usual. Everything seemed to be going well in my particular universe. Or so I thought. We all have our own little universes, complete with an array of idiosyncratic black holes, red dwarfs and the like and we tend to slip in and out of these as circumstance dictates.

At this time of year, as opening day approaches, duck occupy a not insignificant sector of my universe. Specifically 300 of them which had been released on the flight pond in early July. On Friday they reached the venerable age of thirteen weeks and were doing exceptionally well.

For the first time in a number of years, losses had been negligible. On my daily tours of duty around the pond area I had only come across one incident of Reynard's skulduggery and sightings of raptors had been few and far between, unusual because we lose a few birds to peregrines or sparrowhawks. One year a young male peregrine was foolish enough to fancy the decoy magpie in the Larsen trap. Another plus this year had been the fact that a pair of moorhens stayed with us all summer and reared two broods. Moorhens are clumsy birds and always a welcome sight as they are usually the first to disappear if mink take up residence. There is nothing like a good early-warning system!

Maybe I should have spotted the signs. But then again they were none too obvious. Once the young mallard begin to fly they occasionally do their panic flight thing for no apparent reason. One moment they are lazing on the banks of the island, the next they are in the air amidst a whirr of wings and a positive cacophony of duck noises. There was one exceptionally misty morning when, of all things, a wood pigeon triggered a panic flight. I had just finished feeding on the island and was about to leave when the pigeon appeared struggling into the wind. Its line would take it directly over the ducks. Unable to cope with a particularly severe gust, it dived down abruptly towards the pond. In what I presume was an ancient, genetically inspired response to do with hawks and their like, the assembly literally hurled itself into the air.

Then there was the odd dead duck floating in the reed beds, breast partly gnawed away. But there had only been a few of these and their heads were intact. In consequence it seemed unlikely that mink were responsible for their demise. In my experience, decapitation of the prey is *de rigueur* for these thoroughly unpleasant little predators. These casualties, I assumed, were the usual victims of bullying by their peers. They tend to keep away from the feeding areas and literally end up starving to death. Rats, which are quick to home in on any regular scatterings of grain, have a habit of chewing away at their carcasses. All in all I had lost very few of my charges and, as they were now able to fly, there was every reason to believe that future losses would be equally small. A fair reason, I think, to be just that tiny bit smug.

On the morning in question I was, as usual, under pressure of time. Friends were collecting me at 11am on their way to the Game Fair in Birr and I had been rushing to help complete the various jobs on the farm.

Just before 10am I had, also as per usual, waded out to the island in the flight pond with a hefty bag of grain over my shoulder. This was duly scattered around. The strimmed areas by this day of the year were almost completely flattened by innumerable paddled feet. To a casual observer the scene might well have conjured up thoughts of the Pied Piper of Hamelin. As I strode around the island distributing largesse in all directions, and whistling to attract any laggards, my duck were following me quacking enthusiastically as they picked up the grain. At this point in time I am still their best friend.

Having completed the task I had just returned to the mainland and was standing for a few minutes watching the sea of motion which is hundreds of duck searching greedily for food. Without warning, they suddenly rose *en masse* complaining furiously. All, that is, except one. It was standing strangely erect and was being dragged backwards as if by some unseen hand into a patch of heavy vegetation adjoining a strimmed area. At one juncture the unfortunate creature managed to pull itself forward just a little. But all in vain. A large and very black mink leapt upon its back and in no time at all pulled it into the cover. So intent was the assassin on its work that, quite clearly, it did not see me or, if it did, saw no reason to discard its brunch.

So much now for my trip to the Game Fair. The situation demanded immediate attention. About noon I returned to the pond, this time suitably armed. The plan of campaign was simple in the extreme. Feed the island again and then retire to the gorse bushes near the bank and await developments. I had read and heard all about the prodigious killing capacity of mink but I did not know whether it would be ready for another meal so soon. I need not have worried on that score. Within minutes the duck were running around the front of the island chattering furiously as they picked up the barley. And, right on cue, my bold mink once more emerged from the long grass and pounced upon the nearest bird. Once again the remainder took to the air with a positive rush of wings and much alarmed quacking. This time the mink and its prey rolled around on the ground and gave me ample opportunity to fire a No5 cartridge at no more than twenty five yards. The result? Unbelievably, the opposite of what had happened many years previously when I fired at a mink and a rabbit locked together in a deadly embrace. That time the mink fell dead and, quite incredibly, the rabbit took off across the fields. This time the mallard fell dead and the mink slipped into the cover. It seemed impossible that it could have escaped without receiving a few grains. However, when I crossed to the island and searched the immediate area there was no sign of it.

I decided therefore to return to the mainland and wait and watch. The mallard lay where it fell and I wondered, if by some fluke of nature the mink had escaped unscathed, would its blood-lust bring it back to its prey? Twenty minutes later it was clear that this was unlikely to happen.

Nothing for it so at this stage but to beat a hasty retreat and try again later. Question was, if the mink had survived the blast would it have decided that there are easier ways of getting food than darting out of cover when a big pack of birds are feeding?

Twice more that evening I repeated the dose. Around 6pm the dead mallard on the island still lay untouched and, as usual, the duck came over quacking with their usual enthusiasm as I dispensed the food. I waited in hiding until they had consumed all the grain and returned to the water for their post-prandial drink and dabble. No sign of the mink. Just before dusk a repeat exercise proved equally negative. Looking good. Surely the mink had taken a lethal dose of lead! Next morning would tell. Would there be any fresh and partly-consumed carcasses?

Next day I fed the pond as usual morning and evening. The duck, not surprisingly, were a bit edgy but the lure of food tempted them onto the island on each occasion. There had been no further casualties, at least as far as I could ascertain, either in the pond or in the immediate surroundings. As a precaution I decided to strim the entire island, no mean feat this, as the reedy vegetation was tall and dense. In fact we shaved it down literally to the clay. Never again would we leave a place of concealment next to the feeding areas.

There was one great moment when the strimmer was started up. The entire population of the pond took immediately to the sky and circled around for a considerable period. I hadn't fully realised just how well they were flying until that point. Then, gradually, probably realising that the strimmer wasn't going to eat them, they began dropping back to the water. First in ones and twos, then in small packs and finally in a couple of very big groups. In case our mink was still around licking his wounds we set up a few traps baited with fish. I wasn't sure, to be honest, whether a mink would show any interest in them with such an amount of fresh meat at its disposal. No harm trying however.

The following evening arrived and I thought that I could relax. At least just a little. Everything appeared to be back to normal. The duck seemed content to roost on the island once again. And possibly more good news. The traps had not been disturbed. Either, my first hope: the mink had succumbed to the shot or, second best, it had taken its evil little self a long way away. If the latter, my prayer is that someone else will give it what it deserves!

Whilst these events were taking place, a small sideshow was running concurrently and displaying the very real vagaries of nature. Down the years when the pond is visited in the early morning we occasionally come across a very lame duck. Often standing at the water's edge, it will have the most crestfallen of appearances and appear ready to succumb. I have never really ascertained the cause of this particular malady. One day the bird would appear to be perfectly healthy, the next it would seem to be at death's door. Sometimes, I suspect, bullying may be at least partly responsible as the feathers on the back of the head would have something of a mangled look about them. This being said I have never actually seen a lame duck getting a really bad going over from its colleagues.

Anyway, for a few days before I had become aware of the mink, a particularly dejected specimen of duckhood was spending its time moping in one spot, not far from where the mink had appeared from the long grass. At feeding time I would dispense plenty of food well away from it so as to draw away the others and then give it a generous fistful of barley. This it would pick at in a rather half-hearted manner.

The extraordinary thing is that for periods of time it was the only duck on the island but the mink never deigned to touch it. Was it, I wonder, that its almost total lack of activity failed to trigger the blood-lust? I just do not know. A happy ending however: the same duck staged a miraculous recovery and is now flying as well as the rest.

21

The green pheasant

T THE BEST of times, pheasants were something of a scarce commodity in the area. Not surprisingly really. Woodland was most definitely in short supply and the scrub, if such it might be called, provided precious little in the way of secure roosting sites. As for the land itself, only isolated plots were capable of yielding a tillage crop. The few hardy pheasants that did make the place their home eked out a precarious existence in the rushy and sedgy fields that ran along both banks of the river. No question about it, these were more than entitled to designate themselves as real marsh pheasants. And, like their kin in other damp, wild places they believed firmly in the theory that the best way to escape in times of adversity was on foot. Flight, under such circumstances, was very much a matter of last resort.

That pheasants deigned to populate the area at all was something of a mystery. Or, maybe, it was testimony to the durability of the species. As there was no organised shoot within a dozen miles or more, any bird encountered in the course of a day's rough shooting was, more likely than not, one that had been bred locally. Again, testimony to the adaptability of their kind.

The brothers Ralph and Edmund had been enthusiastic shooters since childhood. Now in their late teens, every spare minute during autumn and winter was spent in pursuit of the creatures of the wilds.

In the absence of any formal shooting, most of the local farmers allowed the boys to shoot over their lands. The fact that their father was the biggest landowner in the district probably helped in this respect. Duck were their main quarry. In the early part of the season the local mallard population was more than sufficient to provide for their needs. Then, later, when the river burst its banks, a not uncommon event in their corner of west Wales, countless acres of floodwater attracted teal, wigeon and pintail in profusion. The vast tracts of marshy ground should play host, one would have thought, to an abundance of snipe. But this was not the case. Maybe it was just that the soil, if the ground deserved such accolade, was waterlogged for too long each year and, in consequence, devoid of earthworms and other succulent invertebrates.

Probably because they were so scarce, pheasants had an almost magnetic attraction for the brothers. Sometimes they would become aware of one because it made the fatal mistake of crowing in alarm when, in the gathering dusk, they passed too near its roosting quarters. Sometimes they would get a tip off from a farmhand. Best of all though was Gareth, the local postman. In return for a couple of brace in the course of the season he kept them well informed as to the wanderings of any birds on his extensive round. Sharp eyed, and a first class naturalist, there was little to do with wildlife that escaped Gareth's attention on his daily journey along a few highways and a multitude of byways.

It was a particularly grey evening in early December that Ralph first became aware of what he took to be a new and strange pheasant. He was making his way down to a promising-looking flash left behind by the receding flood when he met the newcomer. Unusually Edmund was not accompanying him on this particular occasion. A disagreeable visit to the dentist earlier in the day had resulted in him being confined to barracks, feeling rather sorry for himself.

As Ralph walked through a rushy patch some hundred yards from the flash, what he thought was an almost black cock pheasant ran out and legged it across the field. However, recounting the event to his brother later that evening, he began to doubt what he had seen. Or thought he had seen. Edmund, still a touch grumpy after his encounter with the dentist, had ridiculed his story. 'You must have been dreaming,' he snapped, 'it was probably a moorhen or a coot that you disturbed.' So vehement in fact was his brother's retort that Ralph concluded that he had been mistaken. He had to admit to himself that he had never seen a pheasant of this colour. Nor, for that matter, had he ever read about one.

There the matter might have ended had it not been for postman Gareth. Calling at the house a few days later he told the brothers that he had seen a very unusual pheasant crossing the road in front of his van. 'I can't be sure,' he said, 'it all happened so quickly, but I'm nearly certain that it was a very dark green!' This was more than enough to galvanize the intrepid pair into action. Black, green or whatever, the bird had clearly taken up residence near the river. That afternoon they searched the place high and low yet, despite the best efforts of their setters, they failed to flush anything save a single snipe.

The better part of a week was to pass before they had time to go in search of the mystery bird once more. This time they had more luck. Relatively speaking that is. As one of the setters entered a small stand of stunted birches, a handsome green pheasant emerged only to disappear again into one of the numerous overgrown drains that crisscrossed the field. 'Told you so,' said Ralph triumphantly to the unbeliever. The setters were immediately ordered into the drain. Hardly had they entered it however when, with a defiant bout of cackling, the object of their quest rose from the far end nearly two hundred yards away. It then proceeded to fly across the river to safety.

Curious to learn more about this unusual bird, the like of which they had never before come across, Ralph and Edmund paid a visit to the local library the following day. There, they quickly discovered, green cock pheasants were not the rarities they had assumed them to be. There were Green Japanese pheasants that had been brought to England during the latter years of the nineteenth century. Most of them had been kept in captivity in collections. Inevitably, however, some eventually escaped and by the second decade of the twentieth century were breeding in the wilds. There was also, they learned, a dark green melanistic bird which, more likely than not, carried some of the genes of the Japanese pheasants. The brothers also discovered that afternoon that melanistic hens are generally darker and redder than those of the more common races. In fact, as Ralph later remarked, it was almost certainly one of these hens that had had the misfortune to cross their path a couple of years previously. On that particular day it had been bright and sunny and the two boys were more than surprised when, having shot what they believed to be a cock, the dog presented them with a very brightly coloured hen.

Where this particular green cock had come from provided something of a puzzle. They knew that pheasants have a habit of wandering, especially around the tail end of the year when food supplies in the wilds are dwindling fast. But it had never really occurred to them just how far some birds were capable of wandering. At a conservative estimate this particular one had travelled at least ten miles for what, quite clearly, was going to be the most dubious of privileges of ending up in their territory.

Anyway, Ralph and Edmund were now firmly focussed. Come hell or high water they were going to bag this pheasant, each of course secretly hoping that it would do the decent thing and provide him with the shot. As matters transpired however the green cock was not going to give up easily. Over the next few weeks the brothers encountered it on a number of occasions. But every time it insisted upon running well out of range before rising. It had, it would seem, quickly adopted the ways of the marsh pheasant when it came to the tricky business of staying alive. In fact, when on command a dog was sent in for the flush, it would inevitably embark upon a frenzied search before setting again some distance away. This performance might be repeated a number of times before the green cock, seemingly confident that it had put sufficient yards between itself and its tormentors, would lift with the now-familiar contemptuous cackle and depart at speed across the river.

It was quite apparent that the object of the brothers' attention was no slouch. At least when it came to the subject of geography. In a few short weeks it had developed a first class knowledge of the topography of the area. In particular it seemed to know all the best lines of retreat. Most of these lead to the river bank. In a typical scenario, when disturbed by questing dogs, it would make its way to the rushy fields. From these it would slip into a dry drain and down to the water's edge. Then, with dogs and guns still many yards away, it would finally take the aerial route to safety. As time passed the cry of the departing cock seemed, to the brothers, to be becoming increasingly triumphal – the avian equivalent of a two fingered salute.

Christmas came and went and, despite having rather more spare time than usual on their hands, Ralph and Edmund never succeeded in getting even remotely near the green cock. Strategy after strategy was devised and failed. Always the wretched bird seemed able to stay one step ahead of the proverbial posse. On one occasion Ralph used a circuitous route to cross the river and waited in a cluster of alders near one of the bird's favoured crossing points. When Edmund and the dogs got it airborne, the wily creature, as if by the exercise of some strange sixth sense, promptly made its crossing a good two hundred yards downstream. On another occasion the brothers again divided forces and hunted the drains up from the river. This time, having travelled a considerable distance from the bank they had, once again, to admit defeat. A hearty cackle from ground that they had walked some minutes previously caused them to turn in dismay, just in time to see the pheasant flying high towards the river.

Fortunately for Ralph and Edmund after a dry spell the rain came in earnest in mid January. Fortunately in the sense that, if other quarry had not become available, the pursuit of the green cock might well have had serious consequences for their mental wellbeing. They had reached a point at which they talked green pheasant, dreamed green pheasant and spent countless hours planning campaigns to bring it to bag. All this to the detriment of everything else.

The heavy rain persisted for the better part of two days and nights.

When the clearance finally came, the river had been transformed into a raging red torrent that had spilled into the adjoining fields for miles on each bank. Countless acres were submerged. On cue, the wigeon arrived. Teal too came in great numbers together with mallard and shoveler. Morning and evening the great packs were on the move, providing the brothers with a more than adequate focus for their shooting. For the moment, thoughts of pheasants, especially one particular green one, went out of their minds.

The season had not long to run when, one Saturday morning, Ralph and Edmund headed for the river bank shortly after dawn. By now the floods had started to recede but there was still more than an adequate amount of water to provide for the needs of roosting fowl. As is their wont wigeon will come to fresh floodwaters at dusk to feed. Later, if the flooding persists, they find new and more interesting foraging places and come instead in the early morning to preen and sleep away the daylight hours on their erstwhile feeding grounds.

The brothers started out along their chosen pathway when, completely without warning, their Labrador flushed a pheasant from a patch of rushes where the water had retreated. It was, of course, the green cock and, of course, neither of them had at this stage loaded his gun. The one and only time when the bird decided to rise within range! As per usual it set off for the river rising steadily over the remaining floodwaters. Gone again! Or so they thought…

But then fate intervened. The green cock, finding itself over the unfamiliar territory of a sea of water, made its first mistake: it panicked and did an about-turn, bringing it onto a flight path that would take it almost directly over the duo. As fine a tall pheasant as any driven shooter would be delighted to encounter. Very little separated the two shots and neither brother could, in all honesty, claim that it was he who had fired the fatal one.

Such are the vagaries of the shooting field. More than delighted with this unexpected turn of events, Ralph and Edmund made for home, all thoughts of wigeon gone. At least for the time being. Later that day the bird was delivered to a local taxidermist.

Now, I am told, the green cock occupies a prime roost in the main hall. From here, perched within its glass dome, it is destined for ever more to cast fixed and glassy eyes on all who enter the house. The price, it might be observed, for a moment of weakness in an otherwise blemish-free life.

22

The evening of the big wind

IT WAS A LITTLE shy of three o'clock and John was feeling decidedly grumpy. He had a couple of days off and the plan had been to devote them exclusively to shooting. January was slipping away and he was not going to get a lot more free time before the season came to an end. Trouble was it had rained all day yesterday, it had rained all night and it was still raining. To compound matters, the leaden sky promised nothing but an early dusk.

He would have probably settled for an evening by the fire if it had not been for the wind. Around the middle of the day, southwesterly gusts began spattering the living room window with sheets of rain. Then, as the day wore on, the gusts became more frequent and by early afternoon the wind was positively howling down the chimney. 'With conditions like this there must surely be duck on the move somewhere,' he thought to himself. 'Only question is, where?' It didn't take him too long to figure out the answer to that particular question. If anywhere was likely to deliver on a day like today, it would be the water meadows on cousin Leo's farm. Sixteen miles away he had, if he got his act together quickly, enough time to get there and down to the river behind the house. It was always, he knew, going to be a gamble. The water meadows he had in mind were exceptionally low-lying and after all the rain there might just be too much water. But the decision had been made and in minutes he was on the road. He smiled as he thought of Labrador Jake. The dog's normal display of enthusiasm when he saw the dog box being hitched up had been conspicuous by its absence. Usually he would come bounding over only too eager to be off. Not today though. The kennel was just too warm and comfortable and John had to raise his voice a couple of decibels to get its occupant out.

To his relief the rain was beginning to clear and way over in the western sky there was the slightest hint of brightness behind the clouds. The wind though was becoming increasingly ferocious. Every gust shook the car and keeping it pointed in the right direction demanded all his concentration. Trees along the roadside were bending ominously in the face of what had now become a full-on gale. At one point a row of ancient beeches behind a high stone wall looked perilously near to the end of their days. What, John wondered, were the chances that they would still be standing on his return? Indeed, would he be able to make it back home at all, the way things were developing?

It was at this point that he realised that he had the road completely and utterly to himself. Wiser and saner mortals, he mused, had decided that this was an evening for a roaring fire and a glass, or maybe two, of a good mulled wine.

Arriving in Leo's yard John received yet another reminder of the strength of the wind. On opening the car door it was almost torn from his grasp. In fact he was fortunate that it remained attached to the car. Then there was the matter of struggling into his waders. This was not an evening to be perched on one leg whilst attempting to stuff the other one into a wader flapping about in the wind.

To get to the water meadows, he had to negotiate a twisting path that ran down a scrub-covered incline from the back of the farmyard. From this path it was not possible to get an idea of the level of flooding as a tall, unkempt hedge obscured the view. The omens though were not good. The roar of the river some six hundred yards distant told its own story. There was no doubt that it had long since burst its banks. As well as this, water was cascading down the path that he was following, transforming it into a tumbling mountain stream.

Under more typical winter conditions, the lower sections of the water meadows would be covered with shallow pools and flashes. Most of these would persist for a week or so after the river had dropped back to its normal level. At dusk they would play host to all manner of duck which came to feed on the succulent grasses and invertebrates that had been forced from their subterranean haunts. Wigeon in particular were in great numbers. On moonlit nights, given the right degree of cloud cover, they were capable of providing quite spectacular sport and it was not unknown for John to linger on for hours after nightfall in the expectation of meeting up with yet another whistling horde.

This however was a very different evening. Emerging from behind the high hedge, John was confronted with a sea of water. And rushing red water at that. There was just nowhere that any self-respecting duck might consider feeding. The question was, was it even worth waiting for the fading light?

If it had not been for the hazardous journey that he had undertaken, he might have done a sharp about-turn and headed back to the car. But, having made the said journey, John was unwilling to retrace his steps if there was even the remotest possibility of a shot or two. As he deliberated, three cormorants came flying downstream, battling into the wind which at this stage had reached, if not surpassed, Force 9. They were just about able to make progress, such was the blast into which they were headed. The fact that they were on the move however finally decided the issue for John. If cormorants felt the need to take to the wing on a day such as this, so too he reckoned might the odd duck.

Walking down to the edge of the floodwater he noticed that there was a strip of slightly higher ground running out some seventy or eighty yards into the field. The water covering it was clearly much shallower than the surrounding water as the green colour of the grass was just perceptible through the swirling redness. At least this would allow him to get a little way out. And there was an additional bonus. The wind was coming up diagonally from the river so any duck following the line that the cormorants had taken would be pushed in his general direction.

The light was not going to last much longer so, ordering Jake to sit in the comparative comfort of a hollow under a cluster of gorse bushes, John walked out into the swirling water. He stopped at a point at which the level was around knee height. Any further and there was the very real risk of two waders full of water.

Not long in position, and feeling more than a little conspicuous in this sea of water, he noticed a pack of small birds fighting their way across the water just feet above the surface. They were golden plover. Behind them another pack of much the same size was following the same line. Neither pack was in range but they gave him cause for hope. First of all there were birds on the move despite the dreadful conditions. And, secondly, they had taken no notice of him whatsoever. He might after all get a few shots before the rising water forced him off his peninsula.

As matters transpired he did not have to wait too long. Shortly after the golden plovers had disappeared into the glooming, John saw in the distance what could only be described as a smallish black blob moving in his general direction. The blob was making very slow progress and it seemed an eternity before he was able to identify it as a tightly-knit pack of wigeon. There was about a dozen birds and unless they had a sudden change of mind they were going to pass him well within range. As they grew closer he realised, much to his delight, that several more tightly packed formations, presumably also wigeon, were intent upon taking the same line. Would they, he wondered, like the golden plover, be so intent upon their battle with the elements that they would not be deterred by his presence? Or would they realise that this strange dark object protruding from the water was something to be strenuously avoided? In the event they came steadily forward, far too intent on keeping airborne to bother with what was beneath. They would, he reckoned, pass no more than twenty yards to his right and at about the same height. Mentally he already had two of them in the bag. But it was not to be. Not allowing fully for the slowness of the wigeon's approach he raised his gun too soon, swung through the leading bird and achieved the not too common feat of firing yards ahead of it. To compound his discomfort, the remainder of the pack scattered at the shot with the wind tossing individual birds to every point of the compass. Try as he might, and with the wind buffeting his gun, John could not line up a second bird. A frantic late effort did no more than waste a cartridge. At this juncture the ever-willing Jake was in the water and swimming out to him. It took a full-blooded roar, such was the strength of the gale, to indicate that on this occasion his services were not required and that he should return immediately to his appointed base.

Fortunately, the sound of the shot died in the wind and the next wigeon pack was keeping resolutely on track. Slowly and steadily they advanced, once again no more than twenty yards to his right. This time John made no mistake. The secret, he realised, was to not shoulder the gun until the duck were almost level with him and then take the two shots as quickly as possible. This he did and was duly rewarded by seeing two wigeon tumble onto the water. The second shot pleased him greatly. On transferring to the second bird, it had taken him all in his power to keep the gun steady. By the time that Jake reached the second wigeon it had been swept some hundred yards away. A slight communications breakdown occurred at this point as Jake, so used to delivering the slain to his master, had to be persuaded to leave them on the bank. The ensuing issue of instructions took place at maximum decibels, such as the human larynx can muster, and caused John to momentarily lose his concentration. In that moment another pack passed by unscathed.

With the communications breakdown rectified, John turned once more to the business at hand. Stretching back to the rapidly-darkening horizon he could see still more packs moving in his general direction. Why they had decided upon this particular line and, indeed, why they felt it necessary to be on the wing at all on such an evening, he could not begin to explain. A few minutes later a smallish pack metamorphosed into a straggly line of seven or eight wigeon as it neared him. As this line struggled into range, he raised his gun. Maybe he shouldered it a fraction early, or maybe the wind played a part. Either way an extraordinary event took place. The nearest bird, the one he had fired at, swung away untouched. The one next in line, barely wing tipped, jerked to its left and succeeded in colliding with its nearest neighbour. It then fell to the water. At virtually the same moment the neighbouring bird, having lost its momentum as a result of the collision, also fell to the water. The two lay side by side for a brief instant only feet from where John stood. Before Jake could reach him, he was able to pluck the two of them from the water. Never before had he seen a bird literally fall from the sky without, as far as he was aware, being struck by a single pellet.

John could not believe his luck. Under conditions which he had thought would almost certainly result in a blank flight, he had four wigeon in the bag and there was every prospect of getting a few more. But it was then that realisation dawned. Putting his hand into his jacket pocket for cartridges, he found that he had little more than half a dozen left. Getting ready to go out a few hours earlier, and thinking that he would be lucky to get a shot at all under the circumstances, he had simply taken a fistful of cartridges from the box and stuffed them into his pocket. Never in his wildest dreams had he thought that he would have the opportunity to fire at least a box of them and very probably more.

Over the next ten minutes wigeon continued to come. They came in twos and threes. They came in small packs. All this in hurricane conditions. Strangely, at least as far as John was able to ascertain, there were no duck on the wing besides the wigeon. On a normal evening flight in these water meadows he would expect a good mix of mallard and teal and, quite likely, a handful of shoveler. Why, he wondered, were they not accompanying their cousins on this particular evening? Maybe, he thought to himself, a slight smile breaking out across his face, they were all that wee bit brighter than wigeon. And maybe that bit brighter than me as well!

With cartridges in seriously short supply, John decided that the only sensible policy was to confine himself to a single shot on each occasion. He had been presented with a once-in-a-lifetime opportunity and it was not one to be wasted. As he had become painfully aware, after a first shot the survivors scattered in all directions aided and abetted by the wind. The chances of a successful second barrel were minimal unless he got the shot off very quickly. Before the failing light brought proceedings to a halt he added a further four wigeon to the bag. At this stage he only had a couple of cartridges left and, ominously, the water had risen steadily during his short stay in its midst. Nothing for it so but an orderly retreat to *terra firma* where Jake awaited him tail wagging furiously.

On the last evening of the season John had an opportunity to make a return visit to the water meadows. It was hard to believe that he was in the same place as on that fateful stormy day. The winds had long since passed, the weather had taken a turn for the better and only a few pools of that sea of red water remained. Would he, he thought, ever experience such an evening again?

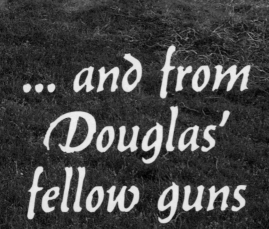

... and from Douglas' fellow guns

23

The man of many tales

by Seamus Leahy

HIS NAME WAS McDunphy but the man in the corner with the pint bottle and the half-pint glass had many of the characteristics of the Ancient Mariner...so much so that he was known by many of the more literary-minded regulars at the *Horse and Hound* as Coleridge. Many a casual dropper-in seeking nothing more than a quick pint on his way home from work found himself fixed by his steely eye, unable to break free. Then McDunphy would proceed to regale him at length with a fantastic tale of his own skills in some activity or other.

If his listener was interested in rugby, then McDunphy told him, leaning close and tapping the chest of his 'prisoner' for emphasis, of how he had brought down a burly Welshman in a club game and when the fellow had protested at the ferocity of the tackle, he had simply caught him up and thrown him into the crowd. That had taught him a lesson but the national selectors were no more impressed than the referee and McDunphy was never afterwards considered for a place on the Irish team. So the story would go.

If it was near summer's end when the hurling championship was taking place he might have a tale of how in his heyday he had held the immortal Eddie Keher scoreless in a club game and how the Kilkenny selectors had pressed him to join their panel before they met Cork in the All-Ireland final. But he was under severe pressure in his job at the time and he could never give the total commitment demanded by membership of a county panel. And on he would go...

There was an evening when a group of cyclists, clad in the latest glad rags of the sport, passed along the street as he was making his way to the watering hole. It was enough to set his imagination alight and by the time he had hooked a listener, he had a tale spun of how Sean Kelly, one of Ireland's finest, had derived his first enthusiasm for cycling from him and McDunphy indeed had consulted him several times for advice during the Tour de France.

And so it went on. There was no sport or no physical activity in which McDunphy had not been up there with the best...and more often than not, leading the field.

But it was of his prowess as a shooting man that he most loved to talk. He told of how he had fallen flat on his face as a pair of pheasants rose from a hedgerow but he managed to roll over and, on his back, had brought the pair down... There was a long day in which he had bagged a few pheasants and in the fading light had stopped to flight a pond. Then, carrying a bag which had him bending under the weight of pheasant and mallard, a pair of woodcock crossed his path and with a right and left he added them to his burden...

'Did I ever tell you about the day I was shooting grouse in the Wicklow Mountains when a covey of eight got up – no, I'm telling you a lie, there were nine in it...' and on he would go until his listener decided that there was nothing to be done but signal another drink to drown the pain of the defeat.

Indeed there were times between the beginning of the grouse season in September and the final whistle of the pheasant and duck season at the end of January that many a patron of the *Horse and Hound* gave the establishment a wide berth. Time was not always as freely available to the rest of the world as it was to McDunphy. And it is one thing to enjoy a well-told tale at one's leisure but quite another when one is under pressure for time but yet feels that the storyteller must, at the risk of insult, be given total attention.

The regulars of the *Horse and Hound* reacted to McDunphy with either amusement or mild annoyance, but his kindly disposition and basic good nature saved him from the kind of response he might otherwise have encountered. In his absence he became the subject of light-hearted chat. 'Did you hear about the latest one of McDunphy's?' and they spoke of his most recent flight of fancy as connoisseurs of the arts might speak of the latest sensation at Sotheby's. Over the years he came to be regarded as a kind of minor institution, as much part of the *Horse and Hound* as the big photograph of Red Rum that adorned the fireplace in the main lounge. Young men departed to jobs in foreign parts and returned to find changes they had never anticipated. They were, however, astonished to find that some things had not changed in the least. McDunphy was still indulging in his flights of fancy as if the world had stood still.

And in a way the world did stand still. Did he believe his own stories? Probably at the time of telling, he did, for there was a quality of innocence about him that made it difficult to see him as a common liar. It was easier to see him, as most did, as a talented weaver of tales, such as one who would have mightily entertained Chaucer's pilgrims on their way to Canterbury. And after all, the true artist must believe in his own creations.

However, like most story-tellers who weave themselves into the role of hero, there was a strong moral tone underlying many of his stories. He had no time... or rather professed not to have... for anyone who did not play the game according to the rules. He had no time for the player who took a dive, the club secretary who falsified a team list or who played around with under-age players' dates of birth.

But lowest of all in McDunphy's despisery was the gunman who did not strictly obey the accepted rules of the sporting life. The man who hunted out of season, the barbarian who brought down an immature bird, the oaf who fired at a pheasant on the ground, the lout who fired at any form of protected species or who didn't play his part in ensuring the maintenance of a healthy level of local stock... these were all creatures who earned the severest strictures he could deliver.

So rigid were the standards of behaviour which he expected other shooters to observe, that a casual gunman who heard him on the subject found himself wondering if it was at all possible that McDunphy could ever in his shooting lifetime have fallen below his own high standards. Many regretted that there would be no chance of putting the matter to the test, since he had not fired a shot in many years... 'The oul arthritis made me hang up the oul gun,' he often explained, never omitting to mention that he blamed the hours spent lying out under the winter moon as the original cause of his indisposition. But he continued to keep a gun and never a season began but he took it down and lovingly cleaned it. 'Reminds me of oul times,' he would explain. And it was known that he had been seen occasionally, sitting in the back porch of the house overlooking the river a short distance from the village where he lived alone, aiming the gun and following in flight passing birds, though never firing.

Ironically, it was this habit of sitting in the back porch gazing across the river which brought about his fall from grace and shattered the image of the shooting man of impeccable moral standards.

A regular at the *Horse and Hound* whose wife frequented auction rooms and car-boot sales became aware that among the lots offered at a local auction was a mounted pheasant. The item was not quite the best example of the taxidermist's art and somewhat the worse for its being a long time since the bird's last flight. Purchased at a knockdown price, it became the subject of much hilarity as numerous suggestions were made at the *Horse and Hound* as to how it might be used to play on McDunphy what was intended as a harmless prank. The plot was hatched, the brainchild of a number of younger patrons who belonged to a generation which had little respect for grey hairs.

The plot was sprung on a sunny evening towards the end of September. Two of the more daring spirits from the pub had undertaken to be the ones to do the deed and, as McDunphy walked the short distance from his home to the nearest shop, they slipped into his back garden and placed the pheasant on the lawn, its base comfortably concealed by grass, about thirty yards from the back porch. They had barely re-emerged into the adjoining field when McDunphy was seen returning to the house and there was nothing for it but to lie low against the hedge.

What they saw next became the stuff of bar-room fun for a long time afterwards. As the two crouched against the hedge they saw McDunphy emerge from the porch, fumbling awkwardly with a couple of cartridges as he stuffed them into the breech. There was a thunderous blast and they saw the stuffed pheasant disintegrate into a fistful of feathers and dust.

The *Horse and Hound* was seething with merriment as the story broke and in the weeks that followed the tale was told over and over again, losing nothing in the telling. The superb shooter and the paragon of sporting virtue had been seen to have, like that pheasant, feet of clay. That McDunphy should have fallen for such an obvious ruse was in itself enough to send anyone chortling. But that the arbiter of proper behaviour should have been found guilty of the two cardinal sins of shooting men – shooting outside the season *and* shooting a bird on the ground – was a guarantee of the laughter being derisive. They could not wait for McDunphy to appear in his usual corner of the lounge bar.

But he did not appear. Night followed night and the longed-for 'Good evening, gentlemen,' was not heard. And then came the realisation that, whether out of shame or through disappointment in his friends, McDunphy had decided that a bridge had been crossed and a step taken that could not be retraced. The hilarity faded and by degrees was replaced by a kind of communal remorse that an elderly man who, after all, had brought a little entertainment and some enjoyment to their lives, had been trapped into making a fool of himself...and all for their amusement.

There was a period of 'Ah, he'll get over it and he'll be back and we needn't make any mention of it while he's here.' But he didn't and he wasn't and then came a report that he was frequenting an off-licence on a daily basis. In time he ceased to be a subject of conversation at the *Horse and Hound*.

In time, too, the ownership changed and with it the clientele. Though the name remained, the décor and the atmosphere were transformed. The big photograph of Red Rum and the hunting prints were replaced by a hotchpotch more to the taste of the young men and their female companions who took over the place each weekend with their raucous chatter and their raucous music. It was no longer a place where even the ghosts of McDunphy and his audience would feel at home.

24

Some adventures of a young shot
by Rupert Butler

KIM WAS a lovely Golden Labrador. Although of noble lineage she never quite got to grips with the whole 'pleasing the boss' scenario: quite the opposite in fact. I remember fondly the opening of the duck season many moons ago when I made the mistake of not taking the direction of the wind into account whilst choosing my ambush point. As all around were, in the time-honoured phrase 'shooting pretty strong', I didn't even succeed in dirtying the barrels. But you will be pleased to know that I left the marsh that evening with nine fine mallard bouncing on my back.

Kim, being a crafty old lady, had decided early on that ours was not the most productive of spots and had taken it upon herself to remedy the situation. During the course of the evening she pinched duck from the water in front of my neighbours, from the bramble patches to their rear and even on one occasion from a game bag. Clever girl. Some couldn't understand where their duck were disappearing to and in one particular case, a fine-looking cocker was getting ferocious abuse for hiding birds in the rushes, or so his owner thought. Kim got an extra measure of rations that night though some others, on hearing the full story, thought that any extras should have been of the leaden variety.

One frosty morning whilst pursuing some long-tails down an overgrown hedgerow I spotted a big old dog fox sneaking his way through brambles ahead of us. Sending my huge golden missile to intercept, I waited for my carnivorous adversary to break cover. And break cover he did, though not in any normal fashion. How he managed it I don't know but he leapt out from a high ditch to the right almost straight over my head and raced away across the paddock. Unaccustomed to such behaviour it took me a few moments to regain my composure sufficiently to loose off a couple of shots in his general direction. To my delight I succeeded in bowling him over. Then, in the blink of an eye, Kim was on him, shaking him furiously, memories of a nasty bite the previous year obviously still fresh in her mind.

On the point of prising the fox from my companion's huge jaws, I heard a chilling sound in the cold morning air, a sound which sent shivers of fear down my spine. It was the sound of a hunting horn. It was not long before I realised the extent of my predicament. I had just flattened the hunt's fox! What to do now? Catching my prize I threw it as high as humanly possible up into a large hawthorn, turned and fled. After much huffing and puffing, and with copious expenditure of sweat, I finally reached the van and flopped onto the bonnet, my lungs in severe danger of exploding. As soon as I had recovered sufficiently I rummaged deep inside the passenger compartment until I located an antiquated pair of binoculars which hastily focussed on developments at the scene of the crime. To my amusement I spied some thirty riders together with numerous foxhounds surrounding the aforementioned bush. I bet the language was unprintable.

★ ★ ★

Then there was the time that we spotted a cock pheasant sneaking into a field of turnips as we drove past. The exuberance of youth. Screeching to a halt we parked the car. To be strictly accurate we didn't actually park it, more like we abandoned it still running at the side of the road, doors slightly ajar, and hurried off in hot pursuit.

As soon as Kim got wind of our winged friend she took off at knots between two drills of turnips with cousin John attempting vainly to keep pace. There must have been a cog missing on the machine that set those roots as it had dropped a seed right in the centre of John's flight path. And from that seed had sprung possibly the largest turnip in the paddock. Why do I never have the camera with me when I need it most? You can probably guess what happened next. Those who have engaged in such madness will know that running full pelt down dampish furrows is hard enough without any obstructions. The somersault that ensued would, without exaggeration, have graced the final of an Olympic gymnastics competition. How Kim escaped with hide intact after this particular episode I will never know.

In her later years Kim developed a fondness for picking duck from a river or channel and depositing them in a neat heap on the far bank. Whether this was the first sign of senility or the product of some strange psychological mishap we had no way of knowing. On one such occasion she managed to stack in excess of half a dozen mallard in such a heap, much to Dad's annoyance. Taking into consideration that one had to hike upstream to a bridge, collect the duck and make the return journey, this involved walking a distance well in excess of a mile. She wasn't the most popular of dogs on that particular evening.

★ ★ ★

New Year's morning many years ago and we were in the lovely county of Mayo for a day's woodcock shooting. My fourteenth birthday had just passed and I had been presented with a sleek, single-barrelled twenty gauge. Our hosts that day had included me in the invitation knowing that a wee chap like me would be more than mad keen to have a crack at these wonderful birds. The shooting commenced and after missing more than I care to remember, I eventually connected, much to the delight of all present. I think the fact that I was starting to get a bit moody heightened the value of that bird more than anything else. Our hosts decided there and then, now that I had bagged a woodcock, they would let me have a crack at a few snipe. Pointing towards a vast area of rushy bog they told me to walk in a straight line and I couldn't go wrong. Following instructions I had not gone ten yards when I sank to my knees in slime. But, being a stubborn little critter, I forged ahead regardless. Some moments later the ground literally opened up and down I went, almost to my waist. Looking around for help I found everybody doubled up in hysterics. It was only then that I realised that I had been well and truly set up.

It was many years later that I got the chance to even the score. Our friends from the west were down for a day's pheasant shooting and I, in the intervening years, had learned how to shoot. And not without some success I hasten to add. Things were going along smoothly enough until one of their number dropped a pheasant on the far side of a deep and fast-flowing river. Our pointer at the time didn't possess the softest of mouths and, on reaching the bird, decided that it was his, and his alone. In a friendly sort of way I hinted that the pheasant might be saved from complete mutilation if one were to dash across the ladder bridge some fifty yards downstream. A ray of hope spread across our guest's face and off he went at a rate of knots. What I had neglected to tell him was that I wouldn't cross that old ladder bridge, not for all the tea in China. With no thought in his mind other than to retrieve his bird from the hound, he was half way across before he realised the error of his ways. This little bridge, having weathered several nasty winters, was now in the last throes of decay. Not unlike a hangman's trapdoor, the bridge opened up beneath him and down he went into the murky depths. As he pulled himself up the muddy bank some moments later I reached down to offer assistance but was told to 'bugger off' in no uncertain terms. He who laughs last... The gentleman concerned would think twice, I felt, before sending some little innocent off to shoot a snipe in a shaking bog.

★ ★ ★

Once when I was very young my brother Owen and I were practising our marksmanship on some sorry-looking bean cans. Being the older he decided to take an extra turn, despite my protests. Eventually, and I mean eventually, he handed over the pellet gun as he realised it was getting to the stage at which I was about to seek some adult intervention. Maybe it was because I was rushing to get going again, at least that's my story, but the gun went off as Owen was replacing the tins. By pure bad luck the pellet buried itself in his backside and all hell broke loose. I never saw a fellow dancing around as much. I wasn't allowed to practise for a long time after that little episode. But I reckoned that it was worth it and, anyway, it was my pellet gun.

★ ★ ★

There is a large expanse of bogland not far from home that, come the new season, abounds with various species of wildfowl. It is the best place I know to get a really mixed bag. On one opening day some years ago I and some like-minded souls accounted for mallard, wigeon, teal, pochard, tufted and gadwall.

The one problem with the place is that, because of the broad expanse of water, it is often difficult to encourage our winged friends to come within range of our ambush points. Decoys work at times but generally the duck seem to treat them with grave suspicion and give them a wide berth. One year, deciding to bite the bullet, I borrowed a canoe from a friend in a local club and paddled off into the pre-dawn glooming, much to the amusement of my colleagues. Now those of you who have risen in the wee hours to partake in such madness will know that connecting with elusive quarry is hard enough on *terra firma*, never mind in the cockpit of a very light canoe. On the morning in question the said duck never appeared in any numbers. Despite this I managed to connect on a couple of occasions, though nearly ending up in the murky depths in the process. I was, however, content in the knowledge that my sceptical colleagues had not got any shooting at all around the fringes. Paddling back towards the shore I was still just a little way out when a friend shouted a warning. Scanning all around I spotted a fine fat tuftie bearing down in my direction at a rate of knots. What happened next will live long in local folklore, mainly because there were so many witnesses to the event. In an effort to catch up with my black and white target I swung too forcibly with the most unfortunate of results. Together with gun, cartridges, and assorted other paraphernalia, I disappeared into the depths. Smugness has a habit of catching up with one at times!

★ ★ ★

Kneeling behind the sea wall down south with a ferocious gale attempting to tear the garments from my back, I remember marvelling as flight after flight of diving duck passed by at breakneck speed, all seeking solace from the ferocity of the elements. On this particular morning, if one were to actually bring one's gun to bear on a bird, remaining airborne was an achievement in itself. Never in all my wanderings in wild places had I seen so many duck on the wing – truly a sight to gladden the heart of any fowler. Connecting with them, however, was another matter entirely. After several fruitless attempts I noticed a large battalion of pochard bearing down at a ferocious pace.

Carefully watching their every move I waited for what I thought was the appropriate moment before jumping up and releasing a couple of barrels. The sheer speed of my swing was too much for my feet and, after a couple of backward somersaults, I ended up battered and bruised on the rocks that formed the base of the sea wall. Pulling myself up tentatively I heard some congratulatory words drift across the wind. Not realising the extent of my success until that moment, I turned to see seven dead pochard bobbing up and down in the waves. After conferring with my colleague I discovered that five had succumbed to my first barrel and two to the second. The pain of my bruised body momentarily forgotten, I awarded myself a little pat on the back. It is not everyday that fortune and misfortune visit one in equal measure.

25

A night to remember
by John Bourke

FROM STUDIES carried out in several countries, scientists have been able to establish that the last Ice Age ended some ten thousand years ago. Furthermore, we are told that there have been at least five Ice Ages in the earth's history. Evidence for this is all around us. Giant boulders, hewn from the earth by glacial activity and strewn miles from their source are but one example. Others include fjords, drumlins, eskers, moraines and inland lakes. In North America, the State of Minnesota, which was mainly sculpted by glacial activity, is known as 'the land of ten thousand lakes'. In Ireland too the Midlands are pockmarked with lakes, bogs and other water-filled depressions.

For centuries these watery havens have proved irresistible to the vast migratory flocks that descend on our shores each autumn from their arctic breeding grounds. This annual influx is, of course, no accident. Our main attraction as a winter destination results from the fact that our climate is strongly moulded by the benign influences of the Gulf Stream. This fortuitous situation literally transforms winter temperatures making Ireland, in effect, the wildfowl equivalent of the Côte d'Azur. But the best part, for those fortunate enough to sally forth in the hunting field as the year unfolds, is being able to savour extraordinary sporting experiences in countryside still resplendent in its autumn glory. For most, the prospect of harvesting a bird or two for the table is reward enough, but once or twice in a lifetime the unexpected occurs, and it is this dimension of our sport that becomes the stuff of legend. As an arctic blast enveloped these shores during 1982 one such slice of good fortune was about to befall a certain young hunter.

To add to the intrigue, as so often happens with these magic moments, mine was merely a case of being in the right place at the right time. On that particular Saturday evening though, the furthest thing from my mind was shooting, as other plans were already in train. With the Christmas party season in full swing, arrangements for the evening had been in place for a number of weeks and nothing, but nothing, could be allowed to stand in their way.

Having gone to some considerable expense, what with a 'state of the art' hair-do and some classy threads, my girlfriend, now my wife, was looking forward eagerly to the occasion in question. Briefly, the plan was that the sweet smelling occupant of a Mark 3 Cortina, complete with black vinyl roof, would arrive at her parents' house around 7.30pm and whisk Cinderella away. Then, following a sumptuous meal, it was straight to the main event and highlight of the whole weekend. To the musical accompaniment of an eight-piece big band blasting out everything from Glen Miller to Bill Haley to Bobby Darin to Elvis, we would trip the light fantastic into the wee small hours.

As already mentioned, during the preceding week the weather had been unusually harsh with biting north-easterlies and iron-hard night frosts. Luckily though, due to an absence of snow, road conditions were tolerable even if a little extra care was called for. As any seasoned shooting man could readily testify, this was ideal fowling weather. The big freeze meant that wildfowl, normally spread far and wide, would be concentrated on brooks and streams and other sheltered areas protected from freezing by overhanging branches and other forms of insulation. For the moment though, the shooting would have to wait. One night of diversion as 'Fred and Ginger' could hardly do any harm, could it?

Everything was going according to plan until a neighbour, who often called to see my father, brought some rather disturbing news. As they chatted over a dram by the fire he wondered aloud if we had all suddenly given up shooting. My ears pricked up. 'Oh Lord no,' my father said, 'though from the amount of work being done around here people must think that we do nothing else. Anyway, why do you ask, Ned?' 'Well,' he said, 'I was in the local last night and young Russell [a serious shooting rival from the far end of the parish] was bragging about shooting six mallard on Wednesday evening.' My heart sank. What had I been thinking about? Here I was all wrapped up in some stupid Christmas party with possibly the best fowling in the locality literally going abegging. The thought of missing some of the action was more than I could bear. There and then my mind was made up, and I knew just where to go. I would take in the evening flight at the Lough and still be back in plenty of time for the festivities.

My father knew that something was afoot when I started doing all my farm chores early and his suspicions were finally confirmed when he saw me putting the gun in the car. 'Where are you off to?' he asked. 'The Lough,' I replied. 'Be very careful,' was his response, 'it can be very dangerous when it's partly frozen.' I hit the road at about 3.30pm which gave me ample time to be in position beside the Lough before dusk. Looking back, going fowling on one's own under such circumstances would appear foolish now but, driven by a young man's passion, thoughts of danger never even arose.

Walking along the narrow track between two stands of mature conifers which leads to the lake, all sorts of thoughts began to run through my mind. Would I make it before the first birds were on the wing? Would someone else be in position ahead of me?

The silence in the semi-twilight corridor of conifers was punctuated every so often by the odd wood pigeon clattering noisily from its roost, indignant at having to leave its cosy lodgings. In the distance, a wily old cock pheasant raucously announced to the world that he was about to turn in for the night as he flew up to roost in his favourite ivy cluster. I knew where he was as we had crossed swords on several occasions in the past. His particular patch was an almost impregnable fortress buttressed by head high briars and blackthorns. It was a place which provided the hunter with little hope of success.

The path eventually widened out delta–like and at last I left the labyrinth of spruce behind. Glancing backwards, the silhouetted shapes of the spruce trees pierced the evening sky and their serried ranks stood defiant against the elements as if to say, 'Throw at me what you will.' Already it was freezing hard with stiffened foliage crunching underfoot. Every breath billowed in the evening air as temperatures steadily began to plummet. Another tough night in store.

After some twenty minutes I reached the edge of the Lough. Outwardly at least there was nothing to indicate the presence of another soul. Could I possibly be in pole position? I made my way to the sheltered side where overhanging sallies and conifers prevented the water from freezing and settled in. Tell-tale signs betraying the presence of duck were everywhere. A positive multitude of feathers bobbed up and down in the shallows. It was looking good. I had barely time to slip two cartridges into the gun before a bunch of teal took me completely by surprise, flashed by and were gone in an instant. They might return, I thought. Then, sooner than you could say Jack Frost, four mallard plopped onto the water, no more than twenty five yards away. This time I was ready.

I jumped to my feet and they were airborne immediately, curling upwards over the trees. I picked the leader of the pack. It fell quickly, followed by a second bird. No sooner had I gathered the pair, which by good fortune had fallen on dry land, and returned to my position, than I was in action again. First a wigeon and then a teal were added to the bag. Then, as quickly as it had started, the flight came to an end. But boy, was I on cloud nine. By now darkness had closed in and I suddenly remembered the Christmas party. Glancing at my watch the luminous hands told me it was 5.30pm…a doddle.

Gathering up my treasure trove I set out on the journey back. I had to take the long way round the Lough and back to the car. I could scarcely have covered a hundred yards when I heard that magical sound beloved of all fowlers. Goose music!

There was nothing for it but to head straight back for the cover along the edge of the Lough. The geese were still a good way off but I had to hurry. I made a beeline for the nearest point of concealment, a narrow strip of semi–submerged ground projecting out into the Lough. It was reasonably dry at its furthest end and had some bushes for cover.

Crouching into this cover at the frozen water's edge I waited as the music grew louder with the approach of the geese. Peering through a small gap in the bushes I could just discern the silhouettes of some thirty birds, but they were way too high. On and on they came until they passed directly overhead at what I estimated was little short of a hundred yards up. Still I dared not lift my head. Cackling noisily and calling to each other, the geese circled way out over a nearby bog and back around again, still too high. Away once more for what seemed like an eternity. Boy, I thought, these geese are seriously cautious. Then, at last, they came just right, no more than thirty yards up. It was now or never.

Charged with adrenaline and with my heart thumping furiously, I jumped to my feet convinced that I would secure an easy right and left. They looked so big I felt that I could not miss. But somehow miss I did with my first barrel. As they tore for the heavens I steadied myself and thankfully connected with the second. The huge bird came crashing down stone dead, straight through the ice about fifteen yards from where I stood. Not expecting to have to make a retrieve from water I had not, foolishly, brought the spaniel. Whether it was a sudden rush of blood to the head I will never know, but I decided to retrieve my goose. No sooner had I left dry land however than I sank to mid thigh depth in freezing water. Luckily I managed to claw my way out. Saturated, frozen and with teeth chattering I had no option but to abandon my prize.

When I finally got back to the car it was coming up to 7pm. It took another twenty minutes to reach home whereupon I hurriedly phoned my girlfriend to say that I had been unavoidably detained. Time then for a quick shower after which I suited up and hit the road.

Taking my courage into my hands, as at this juncture I was about an hour and a half late, I approached the front door wondering just what I was going to say. My diplomatic skills were tested to the full. I think, modesty aside, that I produced an explanation of which any spin doctor could be proud, although I still had to endure a bit of an ear bashing.

Temporarily all was well. Until, that is, I opened the car door. Even though I had had the foresight to put clean rugs over the seats, there was no hiding the smell of the ooze from which I had, not long before, extracted myself. Another lengthy explanation followed. When we finally reached the venue, dinner was over and, not surprisingly, tensions were running high. By the time that the band struck up we were barely on speaking terms. Eventually the night came to an ignominious end with any romantic aspirations taking a complete nosedive. But, as with all good stories, there was quite undeservedly I must confess, a happy ending.

Bright and early on the Sunday morning I returned to the Lough complete with spaniel. Half expecting to find nothing save a few feathers marking the spot where the great bird had fallen, I was more than pleasantly surprised. From where I stood the bird looked to be fully intact. I sent the dog in and in no time at all she was back with my very first goose, an adult greylag.

In conclusion, if there is any moral to my story, it must be all about getting one's priorities right. In mid winter: love or fowling?

26

Memories

by Nancy Walsh

'THE MORNING was intensely foggy with a dewy spray keeping our faces fresh. We had crawled on our bellies for what seemed an eternity in the hope of getting a clean shot at the greylags. But it seemed that any time we got near them a small plane from the nearby airfield flew overhead or the cattle in the next field decided to indulge in a bout of galloping. It was infuriating but exhilarating at the same time. The strange thing was though that the geese did not seem unduly perturbed by these goings-on. At each disturbance they would stop feeding, raise their heads, look around and engage in a little chatter. They would then simply resume grazing. Then, just when we thought that it would never happen, all activity stopped. No traffic, no cattle stampeding, no planes. The geese grazed steadily towards us and finally the magic moment arrived. They were little more than twenty five yards away when we stood up. With a flurry of wings they tore for the sky. But for three of them it was too late. In a couple of days' time we would dine well.'

I listened to the tale with warm admiration. The voice on the radio seemed as close to me as if the storyteller was sitting beside me in front of the kitchen range, bottom oven open so that he could warm his feet. Memories of times past came flooding back.

I have a small claim of family tradition as far as shooting sports are concerned. When I was a nipper I still had one Grand Uncle alive: Michael Collins, known in the locality as the 'Fowler Collins'. Of course he had earned his nickname. In those days in rural County Clare a man heading off across the fields with dogs and gun was 'out fowling'. But, strangely, his love for the sport was not passed on to his sons, or for that matter to his daughters.

Michael's sister, Bridget, married my grandfather, a man with a similar passion. At that time very few men owned or could afford a gun. More often than not it was inherited from a relative. This was how grandfather came into possession of his most cherished possession. Such was his love for fowling that he would rise before daybreak and walk every hill and hollow in search of rabbits, hares and wildfowl. Whenever possible he also shot grouse and woodcock.

There were two small lakes in the heart of the mountains, Lough Eadh Beg and Lough Eadh Mor. It was to these wet places that the geese would come on wild days, driven inland by the force of an Atlantic gale. Situated about five miles from where grandfather lived, it was a long trek on foot across rough terrain. And when he got there, there could be a long wait before the geese came in. In the meantime his small farm at the foot of the mountains had to be tended. Lucky man that he was, grandmother was more than capable of handling the various tasks. No matter what the job, she was more than capable of handling it. Wellington boots, it might be noted, were unheard of in those distant days and sodden leather footwear was one's inevitable companion.

This sort of life inevitably took its toll and grandfather died at the early age of 57 leaving a wife and three young children behind. His son, my uncle Pat, must have inherited his gun since from then on, a single-barrelled one was positioned on two brackets over the kitchen fireplace. Sadly, my uncle did not possess the same passion for fowling that his father had. With the exception of the odd day spent in the pursuit of grouse, which in that era were still quite plentiful on high ground in County Clare, he was not very enthusiastic about the sport. Other than that, only the rabbits and crows that attacked the vegetable patch were likely to come under fire.

And, worse still, his sons had no interest in shooting either.

I'm glad to say however that a love of the gun did not die out in the family. My brother Jimmy was a keen sportsman. As well as his love for the chase he was an accomplished cross country runner and over the years won many cups. How I hated cleaning them and keeping them shining.

Jimmy was also an accomplished set dancer. He was self-taught and I remember him using the sweeping brush in the kitchen as a partner, as he perfected his steps. I often wondered if this might have helped to increase his agility when leaping over ditches and the like in the course of his shooting expeditions. I know that he saved every spare penny in order to purchase a gun. It was his pride and joy and the envy of every young man in the area. By now I had reached my teenage years and would watch with pride as big brother took out his gun to embark on a hunting expedition. On his return it would be cleaned with zeal before being returned to the corner cabinet. At that time people made do with little or nothing and his fowling bag was homemade. Eventually he became the proud owner of a 'real' game bag. Many a fine meal we shared of pheasant, woodcock or grouse as a result of his exploits.

In those days every fowler took some lunch with him but more often than not Jimmy would be so engrossed with the business in hand that he forgot to eat it. The one day of the year which he did not enjoy was, strangely, 12th August, the opening of the grouse season. This was because 'sportsmen' from a nearby town would descend upon what he regarded as his patch. Well-heeled gentlemen like the doctor and the bank manager – the only people who owned motor cars – would appear on the hills on that day, and that day only. They were always immaculately dressed for the occasion and always had a fine lunch stored in the boot of the car. It was well-known that they carried a bottle or two of 'mountain dew' with them to boost energy levels throughout the day's shooting.

There would be occasions when Jimmy might not return from an expedition until well after dusk on a winter's evening. Mother would pace the kitchen backwards and forwards giving an occasional glance at the window and mouth a silent prayer for his wellbeing. Sometimes I would be sent to the 'round bush' to listen for footsteps or some other sign of returning life. Eventually there would be the sound of panting and I would be nearly bowled over by Shot, Jimmy's ever faithful canine companion, as he came bounding over. Despite my annoyance at the dog's unseemly behaviour I was always so relieved at my brother's safe return.

Little did I suspect, in those far distant times, that I would one day become part of another family with more than a passing interest in fowling. My late father-in-law turned out to be a keen sportsman. He was the proud owner of a London-made gun which he kept well concealed in the cupboard under the stairs. During autumn and winter it got plenty of use and in summer it was frequently called upon to rid the barley fields of crows and other pests.

In his turn my husband inherited the gun but unlike his father he had little interest in sporting shooting. The farm by now was largely given over to dairying so in the absence of any real need for crop protection it rarely saw the light of day. But my connection with guns did not end there. Along the way I had gained a cousin through marriage who possesses an admirable array of firearms. Boy, he certainly knows how to use them. And greatly enjoys using them. Needless to say he is always a welcome visitor at our house, given the time I could spend a week listening happily to his tales of adventures with dogs and gun over highlands and lowlands.

After my husband passed away, the gun remained in its 'prison' beneath the stairs for several years. Then one day our beloved cousin came up with an idea. Rather than leave it in its enforced idleness he suggested that we got it decommissioned. It was a handsome thing and deserved better. This was duly done and it now occupies a place of honour over the fireplace in the living room. Nowadays when I look up and see it glistening on the wall, the years fall away and in my mind's eye I see again for a brief moment the Fowler Collins and his like striding out across the bogs.

27

Fiach

by Anthony O'Halloran

FIACH ARRIVED at our house on a perishing November evening. A ball of white fluff, he was small enough to fit quite comfortably on my sister Olive's lap. Prior to that, hints that I was contemplating buying a new puppy had been met with some resistance. As I was away at college for much of the year it was suspected that responsibility for looking after any new arrival would fall primarily on dad. I was also reminded that we already had a two-year-old Labrador and an ageing pointer.

However, being something of a dog-centred household, I was confident that once the family saw this handsome creature any resistance would collapse. So, having purchased Fiach without the family's agreement, I arrived home in a hopeful frame of mind. And I wasn't far off the mark. Once he curled up on Olive's lap it was clearly a matter of no contest.

In the fullness of time the fluffy ball grew to sturdy adulthood. Like many another English setter, Fiach's prime *raison d'être* was to locate pheasant and grouse, something he did with increasing panache. He also became more and more adept at setting snipe. If he had a weakness it had to do with rabbits. Once in a while he clearly felt an irresistible urge to set something of a furry nature rather than the more conventional feathered one. In fairness this aberrant behaviour only really occurred on those days when game birds had the impertinence to absent themselves from their usual surrounds.

Front leg raised with paw slightly curled, tail curving upwards, head tilted in the bird's direction and a motionless partly crouched body, these were the essential components of Fiach's stance. Add the sheer intensity of his face, a very occasional quiver along his spine, the release of pent-up energy when he rushed forward to flush a wily cock pheasant and it is easy to understand why hunters form lifetime bonds with the likes of Fiach.

It is well over thirty years ago since I saw a dog setting for the first time. A pointer with the unlikely name of Sally provided me with the privilege when, in a secluded country lane, she suddenly froze beside a heavy hedgerow. To this young man's eye, the sight of a dog remaining totally motionless, as if in a trance, was little short of incredible. Today I still marvel at the sight of pointers and setters doing their very special thing.

Fiach was undoubtedly the best setter we ever had. With a superb nose combined with a strong and determined personality he was, in his heyday, incredibly fit. Few dogs, to my recollection, were able to keep going as long as he could on the mountain. When lesser hounds could do nothing else save throw themselves into the heather, he would be seen quartering on across the moor as if the day had only just started. To the very end he remained handsome and proud. Tolerating rather than seeking affection, he was a pre-modern macho male. In this regard he was at the opposite end of the spectrum to Rua, an Irish setter we once owned. Rua simply craved affection. He was very much a dog at ease with himself. Fiach on the other hand suffered from periodic bouts of arrogance. 'Leave me alone,' his body language would demand. Perhaps he had always known that he was brilliant.

If I had to put a small black mark against the dog it would be because, especially in his younger days, he had a tendency to range too far ahead. Both he and his master were teased incessantly about this minor deviation. On one famous occasion a friend shouted across the mountain to me, 'Let's buy Fiach a mobile phone so that we can stay in touch with him.' To this a nephew cruelly replied, 'No way, it would cost us a small fortune in long distance calls.'

In somewhat similar vein his concept of staying to heel was, I have to admit, sometimes limited to staying within the same field. But this minor transgression at times had to be admired. There was many an occasion on which we would enter the next field only to find him already setting. With a told–you–so look in his eyes, he would be urging me to hurry on. As one friend put it, Fiach had an uncanny knack of focussing on that section of a field, marsh or hedgerow where a bird would most probably be found.

How would I describe my relationship with Fiach? In my view there are probably three categories of gundog owner. Firstly there are those whose main focus is on bagging game. For them the dog is an indispensable instrument whether for flushing or retrieving purposes. Such owners though, who are fairly rare in my experience, do not derive any real pleasure from watching their dogs working. They are but a means to an end.

Secondly there are those for whom shooting and bagging game are largely irrelevant. Their joy derives from seeing their charges at work in the field. Content to leave the gun behind, it is for them an added bonus when the dog provides shots for their friends. In my experience those who work with retrievers frequently fall into this second category. The sheer pleasure of watching months and years of training come to fruition is what counts.

Thirdly there is the man whose whole approach to the working dog/shooting relationship might be described as holistic. For him the very idea of going hunting without his dog would be quite unthinkable. The dog becomes an extension of his own being. If this man is very lucky, a special dog brings extra meaning to his life. I like to think that I fall into this category.

Of all my memories of Fiach, those that stand out most clearly relate to days on the hill in pursuit of grouse. There is good reason for this. The sheer beauty of the surroundings, the loneliness of the mountains, the odd wild croak of a distant raven and the very wildness of the grouse themselves. All combine to provide an experience unequalled by the pursuit of any other game bird.

My first ever day spent hunting grouse was typical of many, many others down the years. It was a typical mid-September day in 1987. It was also Fiach's first introduction to these noble birds of the high places. The early morning mist was in the process of lifting as we set off across the hills. A light breeze was disturbing the heather from its slumber, perfect conditions for a working dog. Early on I saw a covey of grouse for the first time. In the rising mist seven plumpish birds rose in unison from open ground over one hundred yards away and promptly disappeared from view around a small distant hill.

Not long afterwards Fiach froze. As usual he was a good way ahead, at least a couple of hundred yards. There he was, motionless, near the top of a steep incline. Proceeding in his direction and trying desperately to contain my excitement, I was struggling for breath as I made the climb. Quite literally I kept crouched until I was no more than inches behind Fiach's tail. Then, raising my head just above the level of his, I peered forward. Over the brow of the hill lay a stony patch. Heart pounding, hands sweating I raised my head a little further. There in the midst of the stones were six grouse. One is simply not supposed to get this close to these most wary of birds. In that same second they exploded from the ground in a swirling mass. Fumbling awkwardly I somehow got my double twenty gauge to my shoulder and loosed off two quick shots. To my bitter disappointment not so much as a single feather was dislodged from the fast-departing covey. But then, joy! Joy uninhibited! One of their number appeared to simply fold in mid-air and pitch into the heather. In no time at all Fiach was back with my prize. I held the bird in my hands and marvelled at the sheer perfection of its colours. An old cock grouse, he of the white, densely feathered legs and spectacular red brown plumage. I'm certain sure that no one ever forgets their first grouse.

Fiach is long gone now but of all his exploits in the field that is the one most firmly etched on my brain. If perfection truly exists on this earth then at that moment of a September long ago, I found it.

28

Under a thorn bush

by Rupert Butler

IT WAS ON the first Saturday of September many moons ago that I set out to try a wee pond that sometimes hosts a few early season mallard. Teal too sometimes frequent the place at that time of year. Over the previous few seasons we had rarely returned from this favoured haunt empty-handed. So, full of youthful enthusiasm, I motored my merry way to the farm on that warm early September evening. En route I had called to Dad to see if he wanted to accompany me. Usually he is up for any adventure with the gun but on this occasion he was unwilling to tear himself away from an old war movie that was blaring out of the box in the far corner of the living room. He had not, I suspected, fully recovered from a long and fruitless slog across the hills in search of grouse the previous day. If I recall correctly I was also feeling a bit on the lazy side and it had been a minor struggle to extract myself from the depths of a very comfy sofa.

Reaching Old Jim's farmyard I made sure to park the car in such a way as not to cause an obstruction. There's no knowing what manner of vehicle might be needed in a farmer's yard. Some years ago Dad had, in a rush to reach the pond before dusk fell, parked without what the custodians of law and order refer to as 'due care and consideration'. As a consequence of his carelessness, Old Jim's entire harvesting operation had been brought to a temporary halt. I had no wish to be on the wrong end of such an ear bashing as he got on his return later that evening.

Anyway, I called at the farmhouse door to say hello and, hopefully, to glean any information about the movement of fowl in the area. Old Jim, the owner of the farm, told me that he had heard quacking for several nights now. He was pretty sure that it came from the pond in the field behind the house even though he hadn't been down early enough in the morning to see what was there. A year or so previously he had decided that enough was enough of the never-ending struggle with the land and the elements. There had been too many years of hard toil and nothing but the promise of more to come. He had, in consequence, rented out the entire farm, lock, stock and barrel to a local laddie. This gave him the time and space to do a bit of travelling, something he had often dreamed of doing, as well as pursuing his other great passion in life, namely, downing a few pints of the black stuff. Bidding him good evening I let Willow out of the dog box and sauntered down the lane to the field. There was no need to rush. It was still quite bright and I didn't envisage that even the earliest of arrivals would put in an appearance for at least fifteen minutes. I couldn't have been more wrong.

As I approached the quarter acre pond I was delighted to see that there was no weed growth of any note on the surface. In September, before the frosts come in earnest, a weed-covered pond is unlikely to be frequented by fowl, especially if there are no obvious tracks across the surface. Several moorhens scuttled away across the water as I drew near and launched themselves into clumsy flights. They wouldn't go far, I knew. Once I settled into my ambush spot they would sneak cautiously back.

Walking round the pond, my excitement rose as it became clear that the edges were positively awash with duck feathers. Almost every duck in the parish, it seemed, was paying a nightly visit. I had just reached my destination, a thick and ancient thorn bush which had served me well season after season, when I heard a rustle of wings behind me. Swirling around I was just in time to see four mallard departing at a fair rate of knots. I had no way of knowing whether they had been there ahead of me and had been sleeping under a bank or were on the point of coming in when they copped me. I managed to fumble a single cartridge into the chamber of the choke barrel and loose off an ultra-hasty shot in their general direction. More as a result of good fortune than anything else, one of their number peeled away and glided down into a wild patch overgrown with thistles and brambles. Willow, my long-standing companion on outings such as this, didn't need to be asked twice. In no time at all she came back with a fine drake mallard wedged firmly between her jaws.

The two of us immediately crept in under the generous cover provided by the thorn bush. I had no intention of getting caught like that a second time. My excitement continued to grow. Somehow I knew that this was going to be one of those very special evenings, one of those evenings indeed which remain transfixed in the memory banks long after arthritic legs can no longer transport one to these wild and wonderful places. Willow, too, was that extra bit alert. I have little doubt but that in some strange canine way she was aware of my growing anticipation of events that would surely unfold.

A couple of plops over at the far bank accompanied by gentle ripples passing through the reeds indicated the return of the moorhens. Then the action began in earnest. From high over the sprawling oak to my right, seven mallard came whiffling in. Clearly they were used to the place as there was not the slightest hint of an initial precautionary circuit. This time I was more than ready. Two fell, the first as it came straight at me open winged and landing gear down, the second as it flared high in a grim bid to escape. Over the course of the next twenty minutes mallard came in earnest as the light slowly faded. Some came in ones and twos, others in packs of varying size. In the case of the biggest pack of all they swept in without a sound and the lead birds were on the verge of landing before I could open fire. As can so easily happen under such circumstances my shooting ranged from the brilliant (though I say it myself) to the downright terrible. But the heap of slain birds by my side rose steadily and there was no doubt that Willow was earning her keep. At one point I had to make a quick dash for the car to replenish my dwindling supply of ammo. Not for a single moment had I expected a flight quite like this. On more than one occasion two packs were circling at the same time. Hard to keep the cool under such circumstances. Unusually the teal did not come until quite late. The light had nearly gone and some landed unnoticed by me, only to betray their presence by their chorus of high pitched piping. To be quite honest my cartridge-to-kill ratio for these little latecomers was nowhere near as good as that for their larger cousins.

Finally darkness brought an end to the proceedings. As I got up to go, mallard that I had not even seen coming in rose from the far side of the pond and departed, quacking noisily. It took two trips to transport my birds to the car. Seventeen mallard and four teal: a fine bag for a single gun by any standards and one I doubt that I will ever be lucky enough to get anywhere remotely near again. There are those that criticise bags of this magnitude. But it is my view that they must be seen in context. Everything balances out in the course of a season. There will be plenty of evenings when there is not so much as a single murmur of wings in the darkening sky and the services of the dog are not called upon. As far as I'm concerned gift horses are exceptionally rare creatures and one should not look at whatever part of them one is not supposed to look at.

On the way home I made a detour to Dad's house and invited him out to inspect the contents of the car boot. Even today I can still see his jaw drop in disbelief. Such moments are to be treasured.

29

Now – tell me again – why you were naked with that Labrador?

by Michael Gately

I SUPPOSE many different countries have an area that locals claim to have the finest wildfowling in the world. Let me add the Wexford Sloblands to those rose-tinted claims.

Wexford harbour is the shape of a giant east-facing horseshoe with the Sloblands occupying both the north and south crescents of the horseshoe. I feel myself to be one of the luckiest sportsmen in the world to live on the North Slob, or to be very exact, some seventy five feet off it.

The North Slob is a 2000 acre lowland reclaimed from the sea in the early 1800s. A three mile Dutch-style dyke keeps the sea at bay and the original steam pump has now been replaced by an electric one. This pump controls the level of water in the miles of canals that meander through the Slob. These canals vary considerably in width, some are no more than a few feet, others over a hundred yards. During periods of heavy winter rain, the water level can rise by several feet to a point at which I begin to wonder if more of the

Slob is under water rather than over it. I often console my wife, 'she who prefers the dogs,' with the fact that we will have a beachfront property if the water levels rise any more. One year, after particularly heavy rain, my young ducks simply swam over the top of their release pen and gave me a lot of extra work feeding a much broader area than usual. But, as the saying goes, every cloud has a silver lining. The extra feeding programme paid a handsome dividend later in the season, especially with teal.

Each year over fifty per cent of the world population of Greenland White-fronted geese winter on the Slobs. The great majority of these now favour the North Slob whereas in times past they were fairly evenly distributed over the two polders. Large numbers of Brent geese, Whooper swans and over a dozen species of duck are also present during the autumn and winter months. A visitor centre is open daily and is well worth an hour or so of one's time. Here one can find a fascinating range of information about wildfowl. Did you know, for example, that wigeon can live to be twenty years of age? If you want to see the great skeins of White-fronts, make sure that you come no later than early April. By May they have gone back to Greenland, spending a short holiday in Iceland on the way.

Unfortunately goose shooting is no longer permissible in Wexford despite the hard work of people such as Des Lett, a prominent member of Wexford's amphibious Lett family. It is simply mouth-watering to see skein after skein pass over my house. I'm sure my dogs are now conditioned to ignore the geese whilst watching everything else that moves.

Now, while reminded of my dogs, I want to share a toe-curling secret of mine.

'She who prefers dogs,' had organised one of our regular evening-out torture sessions to which she seems to greatly enjoy subjecting me. So the dogs and I decided that we would cram in our retrieving training in the spare half hour whilst 'She who...' applied the first coat of war paint.

I grabbed my plastic paint can lids and made for the main

channel preceded by half a dozen of my dogs. Yes: I recommend the use of large paint can lids as a retriever training tool. Any professional painter will give you all you need of these for nothing; they tend to be about sixteen inches in diameter and a lot of them are a bright orange colour.

The reason that they are so useful for this particular exercise is that they can be 'Frisbee-d' a long way out and, all-important, they float just below the surface of the water. From the height of a human being, they can be seen at all times whilst they are not visible to a swimming dog until it literally bumps into one of them. Their usefulness therefore lies in the fact your dogs must trust, and continue to build trust, in the directions that you give them. Blind retrieves are thus the main focus and these can be worked on without the painful necessity of having to hide dummies in advance. One is provided with a lot of training choices. For example, a dog can be turned away from a particular blind retrieve and directed towards another of the lids among those scattered around. What's more, it is possible to toss the lids through the air slowly, thus making it easy to convince a young dog of the direction to take before it graduates to full blind retrieving.

But before I get completely carried away with talk of training I must return to my account of that particular rushed session. We arrived at the channel and I started as usual by flying the lids in all directions. The dogs were then sent out in turn, ensuring that the retrieve always came straight to hand.

I suppose it was because I was under pressure of time that I failed to notice a small float from an eel net some distance away on the far side of the channel. Any floating marker like this can be deadly for dogs so it is vital to keep one's eyes open. My Labrador, Jameson, a monster animal though not the world's smartest dog, accidentally picked up the float and, in so doing, had succeeded in getting himself thoroughly tangled in some ropes. A bout of frightened splashing ensued but all my calls to release the float fell on deaf ears. I then tried walking away in the hope that he would work himself free. This didn't work and the whimpering of the terrified dog soon brought me back to the bank.

What was I to do? The Slob is an exceptionally quiet place and if I went in search of help I was afraid that he would become further entangled in the net and would drown before I could make my return. I ran to a nearby jeep thinking that I could grab the spare wheel and use it to keep me afloat if I ventured out and also ended up entangled in the ropes. I had read somewhere that an ordinary car wheel can keep a number of people afloat. It soon became apparent though that it would take too long to undo the nuts which held the spare onto the jeep. Nothing for it so but to strip off and jump in.

Now the Slob is no place to go swimming. There is considerable variation in depth from point to point. As well as this there are parts in which the bottom is covered with a dangerous accumulation of slime. Upon reaching Jameson I realised that I had an even bigger problem on my hands than I had thought. He began rearing up out of the water, way above my head, as he tried to come to me whilst still dragging the net. Treading water I waited for him to turn his back so that I could attempt to free him. Thankfully I got my chance and it did not take too long to extract the terrified creature from the tangle of net and ropes. We were then both able, just, to swim to the bank and scramble ashore.

There we were, a large Labrador shaking on all fours and me in my day of birth glory. I must have looked like that famous sculpture of the thinker, naked with my forehead on my fist. Because we had only one problem now. We were on the wrong bank. To get back to the house without crossing the channel would take me through a lot of unfriendly territory. And I didn't want to be charged with naked trespass. Just think of it. The judge asking, 'Tell me again why you were naked in that secluded area with a very scared dog!'

Weighing up my options did not take too long. I pushed Jameson back into the channel and in 'Old West' river crossing style, steered him to the other bank.

I could swear that the cackle of the ducks as I emerged for the second time from the water was laughter. Listen next time you hear a raucous duck call and you will know what I mean.

Arriving back at the house I hit the shower, dressed and was ready for action before 'She who...' had finished refurbishing herself. Now what does that tell you? Prayers to St Jude please.

30

The first of many
by Anthony O'Halloran

AS A WILDLIFE HABITAT, it could fittingly be described as a Mecca. A combination of marshy ground, thick hedgerows and ditches bearing ivy-covered trees of every kind, this was unquestionably young John's favourite place. Though little more than thirty acres in extent, its small size was compensated for by the quality and diversity of the shooting it could provide.

Late evenings were a favoured time for John to visit. At that hour snipe were likely to explode in abundance from the reed beds. Wood pigeons would burst from the trees and pheasants were likely to be found skulking in the covers on the drier sections. Late in the year an overflowing well became a temporary stream acting as a magnet for mallard and teal alike.

But this place was not without its challenges. A lack of familiarity with the marshy areas could prove dangerous in the extreme. An undisciplined dog could wreak havoc on the most carefully laid plans. In a worst case scenario mallard, pheasant, teal and snipe might all be in the air together. And all out of range.

The main problem however was that John was spoiled for choice. A single shot at a fast-departing cock pheasant at the marsh's edge could, for example, result in the frustrating sight of thirty or so mallard rising eighty yards ahead. Or, there again, a decision to focus solely on duck might bring John to a stream devoid of fowl having left a pheasant or two go unsaluted as he approached. In similar vein, darting snipe might be granted safe passage only for pheasant and duck to be conspicuous by their absence.

Since childhood John had accompanied his father, brother and uncle on hunting forays. His world revolved around local fields, rivers and woods. Since acquiring his first gun at the age of sixteen, he had roamed the countryside with a child-like curiosity and enthusiasm. Accompanied by an assortment of canine companions he was a familiar sight, leaving the village in the early hours and returning well after dusk had fallen.

These were the happiest days of his life. But they were marred by one thing. His failure to bag his first cock pheasant had become a source of considerable irritation. Whilst he had long since bagged his first mallard and teal, no matter how hard he tried, pheasants just kept eluding him. He had been presented with many opportunities including quite straightforward going away birds. He had listened carefully to his father's advice on mounting and lead. All to no avail. Time and time again he was met by failure.

On a late November afternoon many years ago John was accompanied on a hunting trip by his father, Patrick, and his uncle Davy. They had decided to end the day's sport in his favourite place. They had had little success so far and hoped that this final venue would see a reverse in their fortunes. But try as they might they could not flush so much as a single bird. One last throw of the dice remained, the very thickest of the double ditches. Dogs and guns approached eagerly. A light wind rustled the ivy and the branches. Blackbirds made their usual noisy departure as the dogs went about their business. Without success the dogs searched and searched. 'No scent,' said Davy. 'Not a whiff,' replied Patrick. Perhaps it had been hunted earlier in the day, the teenage John mused.

The trio were about to throw in the towel when, some thirty yards ahead, a cock pheasant burst out high above the cover. Crowing belligerently it followed the centre of the double ditch rather than coming out to the guns. Startled, John got a brief glimpse of the fast-departing bird, swung his over and under up instinctively and squeezed the trigger. The cock fell stone dead. At least that is what he thought. Joy and elation quickly turned to bitter disappointment when the Labrador failed to bring the bird to hand. Perhaps, John thought, he had been mistaken. Maybe the cock had been barely clipped and had taken off on foot. This though seemed increasingly unlikely as none of the dogs seemed to pick up even the slightest scent. It was as if the cock had totally disappeared.

For John the journey back to the car was one of utter desolation. Both father and uncle felt for him. His dream of arriving back into the kitchen and proudly displaying his first cock pheasant had been cruelly dashed. Totally convinced that the bird had fallen lifeless, John was certain sure that the Gods had conspired to rob him of a very special moment.

School beckoned the following morning but John's mind was far removed from matters academic. Conscious of his son's very real disappointment, his father took him aside before he left and promised that he would give the double ditch another search.

In school there was the usual Monday morning atmosphere: another week of unwelcome lessons and teachers assigning too much homework. John's mind, as usual, was focussed on shooting and, in particular, the mini tragedy of the previous evening. He could not get it out of his mind. He hoped, he prayed that his father would find that pheasant for him.

Somehow the French Revolution seemed totally irrelevant. Why did he have to listen to such stuff? 'John, just what are you thinking about?' a frustrated teacher of history roared at him. Telling a bare-faced lie he replied, 'Sorry sir, I was wondering if Marie Antoinette could really be as cruel as history depicts her.' Little did that teacher realise that one day John too would become a teacher.

On the bus journey home John, as was his habit, scanned the countryside for game. Sure enough only a mile or so outside the village he spotted two cock pheasants in a stubble field. This information would be immediately relayed to his father on his return. The gloom of the past 24 hours was just beginning to lift as his thoughts turned to next weekend. And the Christmas holidays were just around the corner, with more time for shooting.

Arriving back in the village he set out on the mile long walk to his home in a more upbeat mood. Next weekend, next weekend, he pondered. Perhaps the promised heavy rain might bring in a few wigeon. Heading for the back door of the house he noticed that the garage door was ajar. And hanging from a rafter were two cock pheasants. 'Dad, Dad,' yelled John as he ran into the kitchen. The beaming smile on his father's face was all the confirmation that he needed.

As promised Patrick had returned to the double ditch that afternoon. A search of the spot where John was convinced that the pheasant had fallen had led to success. The bird was literally caught up in heavy brambles a good number of feet above the ground. With the aid of a broken branch Patrick had, not without considerable difficulty, managed to retrieve it. On the way back to the car a cock pheasant was flushed by Sticks, the family dropper. A second bird for the bag and Patrick reflected on the fact that tenacity is the true friend of the game shooter.

Young John is now in his mid-forties and Patrick has reached his 86th year. Davy, alas, is no longer with us. He passed away ten years ago on 1st November, the opening day of the pheasant season. Sadly, John's favourite place now only exists in memory. The double ditches have been bulldozed away and the marshy areas have been drained. Barren and bare, that favourite place is no more.

Also published by Merlin Unwin Books

Rough Shooting in Ireland
Douglas Butler £20

Wild Duck and their pursuit
Douglas Butler £20

Private Thoughts from a Small Shoot
Laurence Catlow £17.99

That Strange Alchemy
Pheasants, trout and a middle-aged man
Laurence Catlow £17.99

The Black Grouse
Patrick Laurie £20

Geese!
Memoirs of a Wildfowler
Edward Miller £20

The Airgun Hunter's Year
Ian Barnett £20

Advice from a Gamekeeper
John Cowan £20

Vintage Guns for the Modern Shot
Diggory Hadoke £30

The British Boxlock Gun & Rifle
Diggory Hadoke £30

The Shootingman's Bedside Book
BB £18.95